HOTSPOTS
TENER

Written and researched by Lindsay Hunt, updated by Els de Vries

Published by Thomas Cook Publishing
A division of Thomas Cook Tour Operations Limited
Company registration no. 1450464 England
The Thomas Cook Business Park, Unit 9, Coningsby Road,
Peterborough PE3 8SB, United Kingdom
Email: books@thomascook.com, Tel: + 44 (0) 1733 416477
www.thomascookpublishing.com

Produced by Cambridge Publishing Management Limited
Burr Elm Court, Main Street, Caldecote CB23 7NU

ISBN: 978-1-84157-860-6

First edition © 2006 Thomas Cook Publishing
This second edition © 2008
Text © Thomas Cook Publishing
Maps © Thomas Cook Publishing/PCGraphics (UK) Limited

Project Editor: Karen Fitzpatrick
Production/DTP: Steven Collins

Printed and bound in Spain by GraphyCems

Cover photography © Thomas Cook

Although every care has been taken in compiling this publication, and the contents
are believed to be correct at the time of printing, Thomas Cook Tour Operations
Limited cannot accept any responsibility for errors or omissions, however caused,
or for changes in details given in the guidebook, or for the consequences of any
reliance on the information provided. Descriptions and assessments are based on
the author's views and experiences when writing and do not necessarily represent
those of Thomas Cook Tour Operations Limited.

CONTENTS

WHAT'S IN YOUR GUIDEBOOK?

Independent authors Impartial, up-to-date information from our travel experts who meticulously source local knowledge.

Experience Thomas Cook's 165 years in the travel industry and guidebook publishing enriches every word with expertise you can trust.

Travel know-how Contributions by thousands of staff around the globe, each one living and breathing travel.

Editors Travel-publishing professionals, pulling everything together to craft a perfect blend of words, pictures, maps and design.

You, the traveller We deliver a practical, no-nonsense approach to information, geared to how you really use it.

● *Houses clinging to the rocks in Masca*

Spain

Morocco

Tenerife

Atlantic Ocean

Puerto de la Cruz
Loro Parque
Los Realejos
La Guancha

Casa de la Cultura & Castillo de San Miguel
Punta de Casado
Garachico
Icod de Los Vinos
Buenavista del Norte
Los Silos
El Tanque TF-82
TF-42

Punta de Teno
Macizo de Teno
TF-436

Parque Del Drago & Mariposario del Drago
El Portillo

Masca
Santiago del Teide

Arguayo
Mount Teide ▲ 3718
Parque Nacional del Teide
Cable Car TF-21
Las Cañadas

Los Gigantes
Puerto de Santiago
TF-38
TF-47
Playa de la Arena
Guia de Isora

Alcalá
TF-82
Playa de San Juan
Paisaje Lunar
Barranco del Infierno
TF-21
Vilaflor

La Palma

Callao Salvaje
Playa Paraiso
Adeje
Granadilla de Abona
TF-51
La Caleta
Arona
San Miguel TF-64
Costa Adeje
Mirador de la Centinela
San Isidro
Playa de las Américas
El Médano
TF-1
Tenerife Sur ✈
Los Cristianos
Los Abrigos
Montañ Roj
Punta de la Rasca
TF-66

La Gomera
Las Galletas
Costa del Silencio
El Hierro

⚪	City
⚪	Large Town
⚪	Small Town
■	POI
▬	Motorway
▬	Main Road
▬	Minor Road
✈	Airport

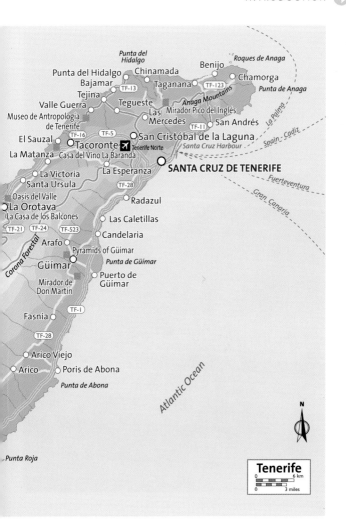

◔ *Pine trees, wild flowers and Mount Teide: the view from Mirador Ortuno*

Getting to know Tenerife

UNDER THE VOLCANO

The Canary Islands lie west of Morocco, along the cusp of the subtropics, about a four-hour plane ride from most northern European capitals. These islands are merely the tips of a series of giant volcanoes that erupted from the seabed over 14 million years ago. Tenerife is the largest of them, a ladle-shaped land-mass dominated by Mount Teide, the highest peak on Spanish territory at 3,718 m (12,225 ft), casting the biggest sea-shadow in the world and often snow-capped in winter.

WINTER SUN & FUN

The Canaries are Europe's closest and most reliable winter sun destination. Of all the islands, Tenerife has the widest range of holiday attractions, sports and nightlife. It also has the most varied and spectacular scenery, from lush banana plantations and pine forests to cinder deserts and cactus ravines – here you can travel from subtropical temperatures to the snowline in less than two hours. Its flowers, wild and cultivated, will fascinate any garden-lover. Even in the cooler winter months, you'll find the island glowing with bougainvillea, hibiscus and oleander, and vivid scarlet poinsettias the size of small trees.

A NOT-SO-SPANISH OUTPOST

The Canaries are a more-or-less self-governing region of Spain, with their own parliament and special tax status. Tenerife shares the administration of the Canary Islands with its neighbour, Gran Canaria. It is the provincial capital of the westerly archipelago, which also includes the three tiny islands of La Gomera, La Palma and El Hierro.

NORTH & SOUTH

Teide's huge peak divides Tenerife into two distinct climatic zones. The northern side is damper and sometimes cloudier, but also much greener. The south is sunnier but the scenery is more arid. Head south if sunshine is your main priority.

THE BEST OF TENERIFE

With reliable sunshine all year round, Tenerife offers Europe's widest range of holiday attractions, sports and nightlife.

TOP 10 ATTRACTIONS

- **Explore the pretty villages of the Anaga mountain range** in the island's northeast tip (see page 62).

- Bask on the fine Saharan sand at **Las Teresitas beach** (see page 73).

- **Climb to the summit of Mount Teide** to take in the amazing view from 3,718 m (12,225 ft) (see page 49).

- **Take a boat trip to La Gomera** Tenerife's small, green and spectacular neighbour (see page 87).

- **Stroll through La Orotava**, a traditional Canarian town (see page 65).

- Find some shade in the exotic green oasis of the **Jardín Botánico** (see page 44).

- Sunbathe and swim on the palm-shaded lagoon of **Lago de Martiánez** (see page 44).

- **Visit the Oratava wine valley** and taste the fine local wines in the *guachinches* (rural bars) (see page 38).

- Make waves in Europe's biggest water park – the newly opened **Siam Park** (see page 104).

- Take a boat trip past the breathtaking cliffs of **Los Gigantes** (see page 33).

◗ *Mount Teide dominates the skyline above Puerto de la Cruz*

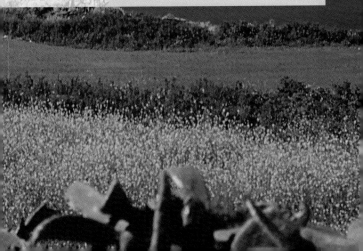

SYMBOLS KEY

The following symbols are used throughout this book:

ⓐ address   ☎ telephone   ⓦ website address   ⓔ email

🕓 opening times   ❶ important

The following symbols are used on the maps:

𝒊 information office   ◯ city

✉ post office   ◯ large town

🛍 shopping   ○ small town

✈ airport   ◼ POI (point of interest)

✚ hospital   ═ motorway

🛡 police station   ━ main road

🚍 bus station   ━ minor road

✝ church

❶ numbers denote featured cafés, restaurants & evening venues

---

RESTAURANT CATEGORIES

The symbol after the name of each restaurant listed in this guide indicates the price of a typical three-course meal without drinks for one person:

£ up to €10   ££ €10–20   £££ above €20

▶ *The spectacular lava pool at Puerto de la Cruz*

RESORTS
Places under the sun

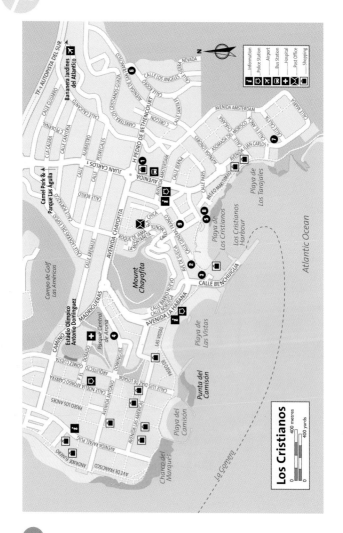

Los Cristianos

Before the mid-1960s, little existed on this arid, volcanic coastline but some banana plantations and a few scattered fishing villages. Los Cristianos was one such village. If you look carefully, you can still find traces of the older settlement behind the harbour, despite the densely packed high-rises all around.

Ravaged by pirate attacks for centuries, the islanders learned to make their homes mainly in the cooler safety of the hills. Even today, the coast is left largely to the foreign invaders who flock here in thousands to top up their tans in the sunshine and drink the bars dry.

The seafront and the 'old town' are mostly pedestrianised, and crammed with shops, restaurants and bars. A plaza with a pretty white church creates a focal point, but most attention is directed towards the beach, where colourfully clad African traders hawk their wares, and impromptu artists sculpt weird and wonderful designs in damp sand.

THINGS TO SEE & DO

Bananera Jardínes del Atlantico
On display at these gardens are lots of bananas and other tropical crop plants, and an exhibition on traditional agriculture and water use on Tenerife. Visitors are offered a free liqueur.

📍 Km 26 off motorway between Las Galletas and Valle San Lorenzo; free bus ☎ 922 72 04 03/03 60 🕐 Regular guided tours between 10.00 and 16.15 ❶ Admission charge

---

TWO RESORTS IN ONE
Los Cristianos and Playa de las Américas (see page 19) are marketed as separate destinations, and feel quite different, but they more or less merge and function as a single entity. Technically, the dividing line between the two towns is Mount Chayofita.

Camel Park

The desert-like landscapes of southern Tenerife are perfect for a
camel ride on this Canarian farm which also has crafts and a small café.
ⓐ 3.5 km (2¼ miles), Km 27, near Arona; free bus **ⓣ** 922 72 10 80
ⓛ 10.00–17.00 **ⓘ** Admission charge

Parque Las Águilas

This place has extensive tropical gardens containing wildlife and birds
of prey. Spectacular shows of eagles flying wild, plus a jungle gym and
bobsleigh rides.
ⓐ 3 km (2 miles) along Los Cristianos–Arona road (Km 27 off motorway);
free bus **ⓣ** 922 72 90 10 **ⓛ** 10.00–17.30 **ⓘ** Admission charge

EXCURSIONS
Island-hopping to La Gomera

A trip to the quiet neighbouring island of La Gomera (see page 87)
provides a marvellous antidote to the bustle of Los Cristianos.

TAKING A BREAK

Kikiriki £ ❶ This convivial, well-priced restaurant behind the bus
station serves grilled meat. **ⓐ** Comercial Apolo **ⓣ** 922 75 30 74
ⓛ 17.00–24.00; closed Sun

Sher e Punjab £ ❷ Good-value Tandoori Indian restaurant; near the
harbour. **ⓐ** Avenida Marítimo, edificio Fontana, local 17 (down the
passageway) **ⓣ** 922 77 78 15 **ⓛ** 12.00–24.00; closed Fri lunch

Casa del Mar ££ ❸ This long-established local favourite near the
harbour excels in fish and seafood, and has won a local award for
top-quality cuisine. **ⓐ** Avenida del Ferry, on the Los Cristianos
harbourside **ⓣ** 922 75 13 23 **ⓛ** 12.30–23.30; closed Mon

Chicago's Bar Restaurant ££ ❹ International menu, breakfast, lunch and evening meals plus seven TV screens showing the top sporting events and nightly cabaret from 18.00 to 24.00. ⓐ Avenida Marítima, Los Cristianos ❶ 922 79 84 78 Ⓦ www.chicagos-tenerife.com Ⓛ 10.00–24.00

Méson Castellano ££ ❺ Authentic Spanish food in a restaurant replete with bull's heads on the wall and a good selection of wines. ⓐ Avenida Antonio Dominguez, Residencial El Camisón, local 40 ❶ 922 79 63 05 Ⓛ 13.00–01.00; closed Tues

Rosie's Cantina ££ ❻ Reliable Mexican food upstairs and outlandish cocktails downstairs in a lively bar/restaurant located near the southern motorway exit route. ⓐ Royal Palm, Oasis del Sur ❶ 922 75 19 72 Ⓛ 18.00–23.15

Shelley's Bistro ££ ❼ Good quality British food including English breakfasts and Sunday roasts. ⓐ Located opposite Arona Gran Hotel ❶ 922 75 12 49 Ⓛ 10.00–23.00

Slow Boat ££ ❽ A popular Chinese restaurant, with several branches in the area. Takeaway and table service. ⓐ Centro Comercial San Telmo ❶ 922 79 33 13 Ⓛ 13.00–24.00

Bistrot d'Alain £££ ❾ Arguably the best French cooking in the south, using the best ingredients, and with excellent service in an intimate, charming setting. ⓐ Valle Menendez ❶ 922 75 23 36 Ⓛ 18.00–23.00; closed Mon ❶ Book ahead

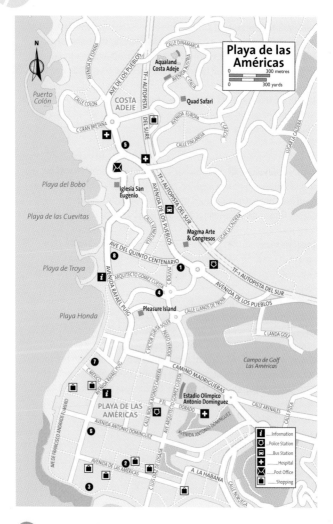

Playa de las Américas

| 0 | 300 metres |
| 0 | 300 yards |

CALLE DINAMARCA

Aqualand Costa Adeje

COSTA ADEJE

Quad Safari

Puerto Colón

Playa del Bobo

Iglesia San Eugenio

Playa de las Cuevitas

Magma Arte & Congresos

Playa de Troya

Pleasure Island

Playa Honda

Campo de Golf Las Américas

CAMINO MADRIGUERAS

Estadio Olímpico Antonio Domínguez

PLAYA DE LAS AMÉRICAS

AVENIDA ANTONIO DOMÍNGUEZ

AVENIDA DE LAS AMÉRICAS

A LA HABANA

i	Information
	Police Station
	Bus Station
+	Hospital
✉	Post Office
	Shopping

Playa de las Américas

As a purpose-built resort, Playa de las Américas suits thousands of visitors down to the ground. Everything you need – shops, beaches, restaurants, bars and nightlife – all lie within convenient reach of your hotel.

BEACHES

There is no shortage of things to do on the long stretch of seafront, which includes **Playa del Bobo**, **Las Cuevitas** and **Playa de Troya**. Most beaches supply thatched parasols and sunbeds and offer water sports such as windsurfing and paragliding. A host of bars and restaurants along the coast provide meals and drinks throughout the day and into the night. For a pleasant, traffic-free view of Playa de las Américas, take the flower-decked **Geranium Walk** round the landscaped cliffs south of Puerto Colón, and choose your spot on the central beaches.

THINGS TO SEE & DO

Aqualand Costa Adeje
An action-packed water park offering slides, chutes, waterfalls and rides, and a magic tap in the sky. Sunbathe while the kids have fun in the water. Dolphin shows are included in the entrance fee.
ⓐ San Eugenio Alto, Costa Adeje (off Km 29). Free bus ⓣ 922 71 52 66
ⓛ 10.00–18.00 ⓘ Admission charge

Boat trips and water sports
Don't miss a chance to spot whales and dolphins while you are at Playa de las Américas. You can also watch marine life through the windows of a submarine or try scuba-diving for an undersea adventure.
ⓐ Daily departures from Puerto Colón

Pleasure Island

Family entertainment stretches into the evenings at this place, with mini-golf, children's entertainers, mini-trampoline, ornamental fishponds, and the fearsome Bungey Rocket ride. There are also video games.

ⓐ Near Starco. Avenida Rafael Puig Lluvina 7 ❶ 922 79 77 76
ⓦ www.pleasureislandtenerife.com

Quad Safari

High-energy quad bike excursions into off-road territory, for between 45 mins and one day. Full equipment provided. Non-drivers only eligible to ride as doubles. ⓐ Parque de la Reina (off Km 25); free bus ❶ 922 71 45 96 ❶ 10.00–20.00 ❶ Book in advance

TAKING A BREAK

El Gomero £ ❶ A well-known haunt for tapas and good Canarian (Gomeran) dishes in a pleasant, simple atmosphere. Popular with locals. Swift service. ⓐ Edificio Las Terrazas, Avenida V Centenario 1 ❶ 922 75 07 13 ❶ Closed Sun

Teppanyaki £ ❷ Skilled Japanese chefs griddle seafood, meat and noodles on iron hotplates. ⓐ Centro Comercial Safari, first floor, Playa de las Americas ❶ 922 79 53 95 ❶ 13.30–23.00

Atlantico ££ ❸ International cuisine in an upmarket setting. Outside terrace next to the pool. ⓐ Parque Santiago 111, Avenida Litoral ❶ 922 79 60 31 ❶ 12.00–16.00 & 19.00–22.00

Doña Juana ££ ❹ This cheerful, plant-strewn Canarian restaurant has friendly, family-run service, well-prepared local dishes and palatable house wines. A word of Spanish gets extra marks. A favourite haunt of discerning expatriates. ⓐ Edificio Playa Azul 2 (beyond Gala Hotel), Calle Arquitecto Gomez Cuesta ❶ 922 79 66 53

SHOPPING

Many of the shops in Playa de las Américas are crowded into huge malls, offering a repetitive range of goods. Some of the best shops, however, include **Parque Santiago**, **San Eugenio** or **Fañabe**. For handicrafts, try the Torviscas market on Thursday or Saturday, and **Los Cristianos** on Sunday. There is a daily indoor market 18.00–22.00 at Puerto Colón.

Sugar and Spices ££ ❺   Italian cuisine specialising in pasta and Mediterranean salads – in a striking black and white setting.
ⓐ Avenida Rafael Puig, Village Club Los Cardones local 2 ☎ 922 79 22 71
🕐 12.00–24.00

AFTER DARK

Garibaldi ££ ❻   Classy Italian restaurant with live piano music.
ⓐ Avenida Rafael Puig ☎ 922 75 70 60 🕐 18.00–24.00 Mon–Sat

The King and I ££ ❼   Thai specialities in a pleasant and less frenetic part of the resort. ⓐ Garden City, San Eugenio, local 12B ☎ 922 75 03 50
🕐 18.00–23.00; closed Tues

Banana Gardens £££ ❽   A fun-filled evening of food followed by a flamenco show and dancing to live music till 04.00. ⓐ In front of Hotel Palm Beach, Avenida Marítima ☎ 922 79 03 85

There's no shortage of life after dark in this resort. Head for **Veronica's**, **Starco Centre** or **The Patch** on the seafront, where over 100 disco bars and nightclubs stay open till late. Sample **Leonardo's**, **Bobby's**, **Rags Disco Pub**, **Waikiki's** and **Brannigans** for a taste of the best.

Costa Adeje, Adeje & Barranco del Infierno

Costa Adeje is an extension of Playa de las Américas, but the two are so melded together that you can hardly see the join. The area just north of the harbour of Puerto Colón is newer and less frenetic than its neighbour, has a good share of restaurants and bars and plenty of shopping centres.

For a break from the bustle of the coast head up to Adeje, a pleasant hillside town with narrow, tree-lined roads and outdoor cafés and bars. Just behind the town is an exciting track that leads past prickly pears and candelabra cacti to Barranco del Infierno.

Bus no 416 from Playa de las Américas drops you right in the main square of Adeje. Walkers should note that it takes an hour to reach the waterfalls at Barranco del Infierno and another hour to get back. Some parts are quite steep, so wear sturdy shoes.

🔺 *The volcanic landscape of Barranco del Infierno*

BEACHES

There is no shortage of things to do, from windsurfing and scuba-diving to sunbathing, on the newer beaches of San Eugenio, Torviscas and Fañabe, which are marketed as **Costa Adeje**. The long stretch of seafront between Puerto Colón and Playa Fañabe is protected by artificial breakwaters and topped up with a regular tonic of extra sand. Most exclusive is the beach below Bahía del Duque Hotel, which can be found at the far north of the resort.

THINGS TO SEE & DO

Golf Costa Adeje

For those who want to exercise their swing, there is an 18-hole golf course in the hills above Costa Adeje.
ⓐ Costa Adeje, Finca Los Olivos s/n, 38660 ⓣ 922 71 00 00
ⓦ www.golfcostaadeje.com ⓔ golfcostadeje@interbook.net

TAKING A BREAK

Bar Oasis £ Typical Canarian bar-eatery serving good tapas and drinks.
ⓐ Calle Grande 5, Adeje ⓣ 922 78 08 27 ⓛ Closed Wed

Catavinos ££ Meaning 'wine taster' in Spanish – this Mediterranean restaurant serves up good tapas or full dinners. ⓐ Shopping Centre Plaza del Duque, local 49-B ⓣ 922 71 73 73 ⓛ 10.00–23.00

El Molino Blanco ££ An old windmill stands at the entrance to this Canarian country house styled restaurant: Canarian food in beautiful surroundings. ⓐ Avenida Austria 5, Adeje ⓣ 922 79 62 82 ⓛ 13.00–24.00; closed Mon

Verdes Restaurant ££ A wide range of Italian and international food, with an enormous choice of pasta dishes. ⓐ Vilaflor Apartments,

Avenida Colón (opposite San Eugenio Shopping Centre) ☎ 922 71 62 15
🕐 12.00–23.30

Las Rocas £££ With authentic background sea noises, this relaxed
and friendly restaurant serves rice, fish and shellfish dishes. ⓐ Hotel
Jardín Tropical, Calle Gran Bretaña ☎ 922 74 60 64 🕐 13.00–16.00 &
19.00–23.00

AFTER DARK

Antonia Café ££ Mix of French and Canarian cooking. Friendly and
cosy atmosphere. Over 40 varieties of French and Spanish wine.
ⓐ Calle Tinerfe El Grande, Esquina Plaza, Adeje ☎ 922 71 00 40
🕐 19.00–24.00; closed Sun & June

El Zena £ Italian/international food in a friendly family atmosphere.
ⓐ Avenida Austria 9, Adeje ☎ 922 75 09 26 🕐 18.00–24.00; closed Mon

🔺 *The busy harbour at Puerto Colón*

Playa Paraiso, Callao Salvaje & La Caleta

These small fishing villages nestle in coves surrounded by dramatic cliffs and banana plantations. Only recently opened to tourism, they are at the moment much quieter than Playa de las Américas and offer activities like scuba diving and breathtaking cliff walks.

Playa Paraiso nestles at the bottom of a winding road, and with only four hotels and a few apartments, it is preparing itself as the next main resort northwards from Playa de las Américas. In Playa Paraiso the choice of food is restricted to international basics like steaks, burgers and pizzas, but further north you'll find some genuinely Spanish fish restaurants in the harbours of Playa San Juan and Alcalá. Callao Salvaje lies near a black, pebbly beach and retains a quiet anonymity with most bars and restaurants in one street. La Caleta, just a short drive from Costa Adeje, makes a pleasant sojourn with its wonderful fish restaurants and peaceful atmosphere.

BEACHES

There are undeveloped black-sand beaches at **Callao Salvaje** and **Playa Paraiso** and a stony beach at **La Caleta**. Most people take a towel and sunbathe on the rocks in front of the fish restaurants at La Caleta.

THINGS TO SEE & DO

Lago Paraiso

A wonderful seawater lido. Great for families and singles. Bar and restaurant, volleyball and children's playground. Also has a first class diving centre, **Barakuda Club Tenerife**, where you can learn to scuba, and then venture out to sea with a qualified PADI instructor to explore a fascinating underwater world.

ⓐ Behind a small beach at the back of the bay in Playa Paraiso
ⓘ 922 74 18 81 Ⓦ www.diving-tenerife.com Ⓛ 09.00–18.00;

● *Scuba divers taking the plunge at Lago Paraiso*

diving excursions, lasting about 50 minutes, are at 10.00 and 15.00 daily except Sunday ❶ Admission charge

Tenerife Pearl

A popular showroom of pearl jewellery, with tea house refreshments and pearl-stringing demonstrations. ⓐ General de Sur, KM 12, Armenime ❶ 922 74 12 50 ⓦ www.worldpearl.com ⓔ tenerifepearl@infonegocio.com ● 09.00–21.00

TAKING A BREAK

Beckhams £ This popular and friendly bar serves tasty food in generous portions and at a good price. Near the Ocean Club. ⓐ Aparthotel, Callao Salvaje ● Daily

Casa Celso £ Good value fish restaurant within earshot of the sea. ⓐ El Cabezo 24, La Caleta ❶ 922 71 01 89 ● 13.00–23.00; closed Mon

Casa Maria £ It's lively good-humoured dining here, with vast servings of steak and chips, together with a jacket potato and salad, plus a drink, all for one low price. Pizzas are not the best item on the menu, but do try the special Casa Maria steak. ⓐ Callao Salvaje, El Jable ⓣ 922 74 13 26 ⓛ 12.00–22.30

Nirvana £ A nice spot for coffee and crepes situated on a sheltered terrace behind the Santander bank. ⓐ Calle El Jable 45, Callao Salvaje

Palacio Real £ Authentic Chinese cuisine in a romantic atmosphere. Varied fixed menus; the crispy duck with pancakes is especially good. Also provides a takeaway service. ⓐ Avenida Adeje Trescientos, Playa Paraiso/Callao Salvaje ⓣ 922 74 17 96 ⓛ 13.00–23.30

Titanic Pizza £ Round the corner from Casa Maria, this is the place for cheap, tasty, top quality pizzas. Take away, or eat on the little terrace in front. Among other popular items on the menu is chicken curry. One of the best in the resort. ⓐ Callao Salvaje

Guila Mar ££ Mediterranean cooking in peaceful surroundings with lovely views of Costa Adeje. ⓐ Centro Comercial El Marqués, local 6 (just south of the lido) ⓣ 922 72 34 79 ⓛ 12.00–24.00; closed Tues

Restaurante La Caleta ££ Delightful Canarian-style fish restaurant also serving snacks and drinks right on the front with views of fishing boats. ⓐ La Caleta harbour ⓣ 922 78 06 75 ⓛ 11.00–23.00

Restaurante La Romantica ££ This romantic restaurant lives up to its name, with tables inside and outside. It serves a good selection of local cuisine, steaks and chicken, with local wines. ⓐ El Ancla 21, Calle Jable, Callao Salvaje ⓣ 922 74 15 18 ⓛ 12.00–23.00

Rosso sul Mare ££ An Italian restaurant/winebar with a terrace overlooking the sea and a great selection of local and Italian wines.
ⓐ Calle El Muelle, La Caleta 🕿 661 33 93 90 🕙 10.00–24.00

La Vieja ££ Named after a Canarian fish, this restaurant serves fish and shellfish in a modern setting with a pleasant terrace overlooking the sea.
ⓐ Calle El Muelle, La Caleta 🕿 922 71 15 48 🕙 13.00–24.00

Masia del Mar £££ A romantic restaurant overlooking the harbour. Serves fresh fish and a good selection of meats. ⓐ Calle El Muelle, La Caleta 🕿 922 71 08 95 Ⓦ www.calamarin.com

Piscis Restaurant £££ Spacious, airy surroundings with views of the fishing harbour and the sound of crashing waves. Serves fish only.
ⓐ Calle El Muelle, La Caleta 🕿 922 71 02 41/08 95 🕙 12.00–24.00

Puerto de Santiago

The main focus of tourist interest north of Playa de las Américas is the expanding complex that includes Puerto de Santiago, Los Gigantes and Playa de la Arena. All three resorts are ideal for people seeking a genuinely peaceful and relaxed atmosphere.

The coastline along this western side of the island is famed for its small coves and awesome cliffs. Puerto de Santiago, a largely British enclave, is built around just such a cove, which once served as the harbour for Santiago del Teide. The resort is linked to Los Gigantes by a walkway around the cliffs.

BEACHES

There's a delightful black-sand beach backed by huge cliffs in the old fishing port of **Puerto de Santiago** which is approached by one steep, but driveable, road. Lovely views from the top.

THINGS TO SEE & DO

Camello Centre

Dress up as a Bedouin and enjoy a camel safari across the hills from this camel farm at El Tanque. Camel caravans depart regularly and you can either stop for a mint tea or get your land legs back while sipping a cool drink at the nearby Bar Los Camellos.

ⓐ El Tanque ☏ 922 13 61 91 🕒 10.00–17.30 ❶ Admission charge

> ## SHOPPING
> Don't miss the Monday market in the main square at Alcalá, or the genuine farmers' market on Wednesday at Playa San Juan for local produce such as wine, cheese, bananas and tomatoes.
> ⓐ Alcalá, Plaza del Llano 🕒 09.00–14.00 Mon; ⓐ Playa San Juan 🕒 09.00–14.00 Wed & Sun

⬥ *Black sand and tall palms at Puerto de Santiago*

TAKING A BREAK

Bamboo Tearoom £ Teas and coffees with a huge choice of pastries. Opposite the Hotel Gigantes. ⓐ Flor de Pascua 25 ☏ 922 86 03 73 🕐 09.00–21.00; till 17.00 Sun

El Barco de Nino ££ Commanding a beautiful view of the sea and cliffs of Los Gigantes, this popular restaurant serves up fresh fish and meat dishes. ⓐ Calle La Hondura, Comercial Mar Blanco, Puerto Santiago ☏ 922 86 83 39 🕐 12.00–23.00

El Meson ££ Enjoy the view from this likeable, popular family-run restaurant towards La Gomera; there is a friendly welcome and good, traditional Spanish dishes. ⓐ Carretera General ☏ 922 86 04 76 🕐 Daily

Pekin Garden ££ Extensive Chinese menu – billed as the best in town. It also does a takeaway service. ⓐ Calle Angeles ☏ 922 86 20 83 ❶ Credit cards accepted

El Pescador II ££ A good place to tuck into fish or meat dishes and to people watch. ⓐ Calle La Hondura, opposite Hotel Barceló Puerto Santiago ☏ 922 86 15 41 🕐 12.00–23.00

AFTER DARK

Fisherman's Inn ££ In a lovely location overlooking the harbour, this inn, also known as Meson de los Pescadores, specialises in fish. ⓐ Agustín León, Puerto de Santiago ☏ 922 86 70 46 🕐 18.00–late; closed Tues

Harbour Lites ££ This bar and bistro, the last one in the row on the marina, specialises in Mexican food and bistro type dishes. ⓐ Poblado Marinero ☏ 922 86 70 43 🕐 18.30–22.00; closed Sat

Shamiana ££ Uses traditional recipes and Indian spices, including special sauces. ⓐ Calle El Puerto 2, below the El Patio bar ⓛ From 19.00; closed Tues

🔺 *A brightly coloured tapas bar*

Los Gigantes

Los Gigantes' smart apartments are attractively landscaped into the steep folds of land rising from the water's edge and accessed by a tangle of serpentine roads. The resort caters for an upmarket clientele who enjoy messing about in boats.

THINGS TO SEE & DO

Boat trips

Whatever else you do in Puerto de Santiago, don't miss a boat trip past the breathtaking cliffs of Los Gigantes. Three times the height of the

⬥ *The marina and cliffs at Los Gigantes*

white cliffs of Dover, these black giants plunge sheer to the waterline, dwarfing passing pleasure craft.

Lots of pleasure cruises depart from Los Gigantes harbour, heading into the bay in search of whales and dolphins; other excursions promise big-game fishing; and there are frequent trips up the coast past towering black cliffs, *Nashira* being one good option.

Centro Alfarero

A small ceramics and folk museum in the village of Arguayo displays pottery made in the same style as the ancient Guanches, shaped by hand without a wheel and fired in traditional wood-fired kilns. ⓐ Carretera General 35, Arguayo ⓣ 922 86 34 65 ⓒ 10.00–13.00 & 16.00–19.00, 10.00–14.00 Sun; closed Mon ⓘ Admission free

Shopping

Los Gigantes is a pretty resort with narrow streets and a pedestrian zone around the church and main plaza, which is also the focal point of the town for the annual Carnival and other big events. It's an enjoyable resort for shopping and strolling, with a variety of good shops, some offering designer clothes, perfumes and traditional souvenirs as well as the usual discount stores.

Water sports

The ritzy little private marina at Los Gigantes sets the tone of the resort. Pleasure boating is a prime activity. Beaches nearby consist of black sand and are quite small and the one north of the marina is very attractive. The water is clear and sparkling, but can be rough, so watch for warning flags.

EXCURSIONS
Masca

One of the most popular visits by hire car is to the terraced, fertile terrain behind Los Gigantes, to see the spectacular 'lost village' of Masca. Until a few years ago, this tiny place was virtually cut off from civilisation, without electricity and inaccessible except by mule. Now an improved road (though still with hairpin bends!) passes through the Macizo de Teno, a region of ancient basalt buckled into ridges and deep canyons. Several restaurants along the main road offer Canarian cooking here; try **La Pimentera de Salvador** for excellent views. En route lie Tamaimo and the regional centre of Santiago del Teide, bright with flowers and a pretty church.

TAKING A BREAK

Bamboo Tearoom £ Opposite the Hotel Gigantes, this homely café serves teas and coffees and a huge selection of cakes. ⓐ Flor de Pascua 25 ❶ 922 86 03 73 ⓛ 09.00–21.00; until 17.00 Sun

🔺 *Evening sunlight on the cliffs at Los Gigantes*

◆ A spectacular view of the cliffs at Los Gigantes

Bella Napoli £ An inexpensive and satisfying typical pizzeria situated in the marina area, the restaurant also has a range of other dishes in its repertoire. ⓐ Poblado Marinero 4 ⓣ 922 86 11 34 ⓛ 11.00–24.00 ⓘ Credit cards accepted

El Dique £ A good, reliable eatery on the marina at the far end of the resort, this restaurant is popular with locals and is certainly loaded with Canarian atmosphere. It serves traditional island food at very reasonable prices. ⓐ Poblado Marinero ⓣ 922 86 72 89

AFTER DARK

Restaurants
Highland Paddy III ££ This is a fun pub, with quiz nights and karaoke, live music, Sky digital TV, fully air-conditioned. Families welcome. ⓐ Flor de Pascua 5 ⓣ 922 86 11 75 ⓛ 11.00–03.00

Miranda's ££ International cuisine with light modern decor. Good steaks and seafood and Canarian wines. ⓐ Calle Flor de Pascua 23, Los Gigantes ⓣ 922 86 02 07 ⓛ 18.30–22.00 ⓘ Credit cards accepted

Bars
Bamboo Bar Los Gigantes' oldest established bar. ⓐ Flor de Pascua ⓣ 922 86 73 77

Green Corner is a cocktail bar with comfortable chairs, good music and a lively atmosphere. ⓐ Los Gigantes.

Playa de la Arena

Scenic Playa de la Arena nestles a little way to the south of Los Gigantes and Puerto de Santiago with accommodation climbing the hills from the seashore. The award-winning beach is clean, sheltered and gently shelving, and made of the black volcanic sand typical of Tenerife. The resort will appeal to families looking for a quiet break and there are plenty of civilised cafés and restaurants at all price ranges.

THINGS TO SEE & DO

Caesar's Palace
Keep the kids amused in this maze of electronic paraphernalia. Games galore and special rides. Children under 16 are not allowed to play the fruit machines or enter the gaming area. ⓐ Avenida Marítima, Playa de la Arena ⓛ Until late

Mirador de Chio
A lovely car drive from Playa de la Arena takes you through inhospitable landscapes to Chio where you can witness the results of Mount Teide's last eruption in 1798. Stop at the Mirador de Chio for breathtaking views of the ashen badlands.

Wine tasting
The wine cellar at Chinyero Bar Restaurant at Santiago del Teide is a great venue for tasting Canarian wines over snacks and a good place to buy your wines, cheeses and liqueurs. ⓐ Avenida Gral Franco 2, Santiago del Teide ⓣ 922 86 40 40 ⓦ www.barrest-chinyero.com ⓛ 08.00–21.00

It's also worth heading into the Orotava wine valley to discover the 'guachinches' (pronounced 'gwa-CHEEN-chays') – makeshift rural bars selling seasonal country wine and fantastic home-made dishes like rabbit stew and goat's cheese.

⬤ *A view of Playa de la Arena from Puerto de Santiago*

TAKING A BREAK

Ninos III £ An informal and relaxed pizzeria serving good-sized portions.
ⓐ Avenida Marítima, Playa de la Arena ⓣ 922 86 15 50 ⓛ 10.00–23.00

Casa El Farol ££ Canarian food in a beautifully restored old mansion.
You'll find local delicacies such as goat and rabbit on the menu here.
ⓐ Calle San Juan 14 ⓣ 922 36 88 41 ⓛ 12.00–22.00; closed Mon

Casa Pancho ££ An award-winning, long-established restaurant near
Playa la Arena, Casa Pancho's has a relaxed informality, a shaded outdoor
terrace, and a menu of tasty Spanish and Canarian food. Try the excellent
desserts such as white chocolate pudding with orange sauce.
ⓐ Avenida Martina ⓣ 922 86 13 23 ⓛ 13.00–16.00 & 20.00–23.00
(summer); 13.00–16.00 & 19.30–22.30 (winter); closed Mon & all of June

El Monasterio ££ This popular restaurant is set in a monastery dating
back to 1646. With delightful rustic decor and friendly service, it has six
dining rooms and a tearoom with a stunning view. ⓐ La Motañeta 12,

🔺 *The beach at Playa de la Arena*

Los Realejos ☎ 922 34 43 11 🕒 09.00–01.00 ❶ Take bus 352 direction Los Realejos (15 min) or a taxi (10 min)

Restaurante Fleytas ££ Canarian specialities including meat dishes in sauce. Excellent wines. Makes a good stop for lunch if you're on your way to or from Masca. ⓐ Carretera General 53, TF-82 ☎ 922 13 62 80 🕒 08.00–20.00; closed Thur

Sala Thai ££ The only Thai restaurant in town; all dishes are prepared by the Thai chef. There's also a takeaway service. ⓐ Avenida Marítima 33, Edificio Princesa Isora, local 4, Varadero ☎ 922 86 07 80 🕒 12.00–16.00 & 19.00–23.00

Sirena II ££ On the beach with nice views of black rocks. Serves steak, fish and meat, strawberries and ice cream. ⓐ Avenida Marítima ☎ 922 86 03 35 🕒 12.00–23.00

Salzburg £££ Intimate and upmarket restaurant, serving high quality Austrian cuisine. ⓐ Avenida Marítima 33, Playa de la Arena 🕒 10.00–23.00 ❶ Credit cards accepted

AFTER DARK

Playa de la Arena has many bars, some with music and opening until late, but few discos or nightclubs. For a wider choice, take a taxi into Los Gigantes.

El Granero is the top name in Playa de la Arena, the major disco and nightclub for the whole area. It has a stage where proper rock bands sometimes perform, and has also been used as the venue for the presentation of the annual Miss Tenerife contest. ⓐ Avenida Marítima, Playa de la Arena 🕒 22.30–05.00; closed Tues

Highland Paddy is another popular disco/nightclub in town. Lively atmosphere. ⓐ Avenida Marítima, Playa de la Arena 🕒 22.00–05.00

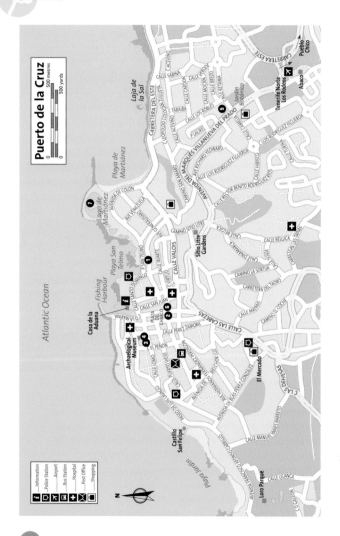

Puerto de la Cruz

Puerto de la Cruz

Nowhere matches Puerto for charm and style. British visitors have long-standing associations with the resort, and love it for its distinctive Canarian buildings and green landscapes.

Tenerife's biggest northerly resort is the oldest on the island, a former fishing village unexpectedly promoted to the rank of principal cargo port after a volcanic eruption destroyed the town of Garachico in 1706. Puerto is especially popular with older visitors, but it certainly isn't staid. In the evenings the old town hums with life and everyone enjoys a walk through San Telmo and the charming pedestrianised plazas near the fishing harbour.

If you want to party, you'll find plenty going on in basement discos and upstairs bars. Elegant restaurants in beautiful balconied houses, a lavish nightclub and the island's smartest casino cater for the small hours. For walks and excursions, Puerto de la Cruz offers many advantages as a touring base, with good motorway connections to the rest of the island. For island-hopping, the northern airport of Los Rodeos is only half an hour away.

BEACHES

The rocky coastline means some of the natural beaches can be quite dangerous. The upside of the heavy breakers is some of the most exciting surf imaginable on European shores. If you walk along the pedestrianised Paseo San Telmo at night, you'll be mesmerised by the bubble-bath waves dashing against black rocks. After a mid-Atlantic gale, it's better than fireworks!. Centrepiece of the seafront is the beautifully landscaped **Lago de Martiánez** (also known as the Lido), an artificial complex of pools, islands and sun terraces built from lava rocks.

🔺 A beautiful sunset over Puerto de la Cruz

THINGS TO SEE & DO

Abaco

A beautifully restored Canarian mansion, with British connections and fine grounds, dating from the 17th century. There is a guided tour and folk dancing as well as a cocktail bar.

ⓐ Calle Casa Grande, El Durazno ☎ 922 37 48 11
ⓦ www.abacotenerife.com ⏰ 10.00–13.30. Cocktail bar: 15.30–23.00
ⓘ Admission charge

Jardín Botánico (Botanic Gardens)

An oasis of tropical plants dating from the 18th century, designed to accommodate species from the New World put here to 'acclimatise' before being transferred to mainland Spain. Look for the amazing giant South American fig (*Casseopea dealbata*).

ⓐ Calle Retama 2, La Paz ☎ 922 38 35 72 ⓦ www.icia.es ⏰ 09.00–18.00 (winter); 09.00–19.00 (summer) ⓘ Admission charge

Lago de Martiánez

Fountains, palms, sculpture and beautifully kept facilities make this lido essential visiting at least once during your stay in Puerto. A modest

SHOPPING

El Mercado Don't miss the daily market for colourful displays of vegetables, fruit, fish, meat and local cheeses. Plenty of parking.
ⓐ Avenida de Blas Pérez González ⓛ Closed Sun

admission charge allows you to stay all day. The sound of the waves just beyond the walls is an added attraction. ⓣ 922 38 59 55 ⓛ 10.00–18.00

Loro Parque

The world's largest parrot collection, plus dolphins, sea lions and other animals in beautifully landscaped grounds. A thoroughly entertaining day out. ⓐ Avenida Loro Parque; free train from Avenida de Colón ⓣ 922 37 38 41 ⓦ www.loroparque.com ⓛ 08.30–18.45 ❶ Admission charge

Pueblo Chico

This model park features the Canary Islands in miniature.
ⓐ Camino Cruz de los Martillos 62 ⓣ 922 33 40 60
ⓦ www.pueblochico.com ⓛ 09.00–18.00 ❶ Bus 353 or 350 from Puerto de la Cruz

Sitio Litre Gardens

Orchids and a fine dragon tree in a British-owned private mansion garden dating from the 18th century. Try the café for freshly squeezed fruit juices. Canarian wines on sale.
ⓐ Camino Sitio Litre ⓣ 922 38 24 17 ⓛ 09.30–17.00 ❶ Admission charge

TAKING A BREAK

Rancho Grande £ ❶ An atmospheric seafront setting for homecooked cakes, snacks or drinks. The balcony tables have fantastic views of the town. ⓐ Paseo San Telmo 10 ⓣ 922 38 37 52
ⓛ 09.00–01.00

Café Dynamico ££ ❷ Sit back and have a coffee or nibble at snacks in the shade at this welcoming outdoor café right in the middle of the square. ⓐ Plaza del Charco, near the fishing harbour ⓣ 922 37 38 95

La Papaya ££ ❸ A lovely Canarian building in the old town offers generous helpings of local and international fare. Garden patio. Friendly service. ⓐ Calle Lomo 14 ⓣ 922 38 28 11 ⓛ Closed Wed

Regulo ££ ❹ An attractive rustic interior is the setting for fresh seafood grills. ⓐ Calle Pérez Zamora 16. ⓣ 922 38 45 06 ⓛ 12.00–15.00 & 18.00–23.00; closed Sun & Mon lunch

Magnolia £££ ❺ One of Puerto's most acclaimed restaurants, offering Catalan specialities near the Botanic Gardens. ⓐ Avenida del Marques Villanueva del Prado ⓣ 922 38 56 14 ⓛ 13.00–16.00 & 19.00–24.00; closed Tues

AFTER DARK

Azucar ££ ❻ This four room Cuban Salsa bar gets very busy at weekends but the Mojitos are worth the wait. ⓐ Corner of Calle Blanco and Calle Iriarte ⓣ 922 387 014 ⓛ 19.30–04.00

Casino £££ ❼ Make an evening of it at the casino with panoramic views over the north coast. Very attentive service and polished presentation. The house cocktails are extremely good. ⓐ Lago de Martiánez ⓣ 922 38 05 50 ⓦ www.casinostenerife.com ⓛ 20.00–03.00

❶ *Hairpin bends and spectacular views on the slopes of Mount Teide*

EXCURSIONS
Out & about

Mount Teide

If the weather is kind, don't miss a chance to visit Tenerife's glorious volcano that dominates the centre of the island. A visit to Mount Teide is the most popular tourist excursion on Tenerife. No matter how many times they've visited the island before, many regular visitors still make a beeline for the volcano. Some even spend most of their holidays there, walking its astonishing landscapes.

⬤ *Mount Teide's lunar landscape*

Mount Teide forms part of a spectacular crater zone, which is now one of Spain's largest national parks. The sight of its snow-capped summit rearing to 3,718 m (12,225 ft) above a halo of clouds will stay with you for a long time. If the volcano seems big now, scientists believe it is only a fraction of the size of a volcano that collapsed or exploded eons ago, leaving the 16 km (10 mile) wide crater of Las Cañadas behind it.

From below, Teide appears as a single peak, but when you're nearer the top you can see it's a much more complex cone with several vents. Eruptions have been recorded several times in the 500 years since the Spaniards arrived. It scared the wits out of Columbus's shipmates as they sailed past the island in 1492 (the supernatural smoke and flames were regarded as a dreadful omen). It was last active in 1798, when lava spewed from the Pico Viejo (Old Cone) on the west side of the volcano for three months. Since then it's been dormant, but if its sulphurous wheezings are anything to judge by, Tenerife may not have heard the last of the old monster yet.

Climbing Teide

An unforgettable experience – on a clear day you can see the whole of Tenerife and the neighbouring Canary Islands too. A *teleférico* (cable car) departs from a point roughly midway between El Portillo and the Boca de Tauce, where the approach roads to the park converge. You can't miss it, as there's only one road (TF-21) through the park. Weather conditions affect the cable car; it won't run if it's windy. You can also expect to queue for up to three hours for the cable car: this is physically demanding and explains why many people opt to miss out the trip to the very summit. Don't be too disheartened if you can't get to the top; the scenery of Las Cañadas amply justifies the trip.

Access to the summit from the top cable-car station (a further 160 m/525 ft up, or half an hour's walk) is restricted to authorised walking groups because of concerns about erosion. But you can take a short walk across lava paths round the cone to see some marvellous views. It's wise to arrive as early as you can if you're travelling independently, to avoid queues and get the best chance of clear

● *Mount Teide, Tenerife's highest peak*

CABLE CAR FACTS AND FIGURES
- Max no. of passengers: 30
- Journey time: 8 minutes
- Max speed: 8 m (26 ft) per second
- Distance: 2,482 m (8,146 ft)
- Vertical ascent: 1,199 m (3,935 ft)
- Height at the bottom station: 2,356 m (7,732 ft)
- Height at the top station: 3,556 m (11,668 ft)
- Open 09.00–16.00 (upwards); 09.00–17.00 (return)

weather. Phone the information hotline to find out whether it's running.
🅘 922 69 40 38 🅦 www.telefericoteide.com 🕒 09.00–16.00

Wear sensible clothing, and take sunglasses and water. The terrain
at the top is rough, and, at 3,718 m (12,225 ft), it's a bit chilly. No one with
respiratory or heart problems, or high blood pressure, should attempt
the ascent. Take it easy when you get out of the cable car. You may feel
slightly dizzy or breathless in the thin air. Visitors are strictly forbidden
to remove rocks or plants from Mount Teide as souvenirs. If you're
spotted doing so, there will be serious consequences.

Parque Nacional del Teide

Mount Teide is surrounded by an amazing crater called the Caldera
de las Cañadas. Lava badlands and sandy plateaux fringed by shattered
crags cover an area of about 136 sq km (52 sq miles). Anyone will find
these lunar landscapes spectacular, but the Teide National Park is
particularly interesting to geologists and botanists.

Only one road passes through the park, well used by the million or so
visitors who head for Teide by coach or car every year. If you want to get
away from it all, take to your feet. Not all parts of the park are accessible,
but you can see a great deal more of it on foot than you can by road. An
illustrated map, showing the main places of interest, walking routes
and typical flowers, is available from the information centres, and from

○ *Walking on the pumice paths of Mount Teide*

the Centro de Visitantes (Visitor Centre) at El Portilló, which has a bookshop, a multilingual audio-visual show and a volcano exhibition.
🕐 09.00–16.00 ❶ Admission free

Centro de Artesanía Multivision

If you don't want to climb Mount Teide, you can see it on a panoramic screen with English commentary in the comfort of an air-conditioned cinema at this new visitor centre.
📍 Multivision Parque, Vilaflor, about 16 km (10 miles) south of Mount Teide ☎ 922 70 91 75 🕐 Regular shows every 30 minutes, 08.30 (09.30 in winter)–18.00 ❶ Good parking facilities

TAKING A BREAK

There's not much choice within the park itself, but you'll find places on all the approach roads, and it's a great place to take a picnic. The Visitor Centre at El Portilló has several bars and restaurants, which are open all day.

Parador Nacional del Teide ££ The renovated *parador* (state-run hotel) in the National Park offers a chance to sample excellent regional cooking in its attractive restaurant, or snacks and drinks at the daytime self-service café next door. Picture-windows and a sun terrace capture views of the extraordinary Roques de García. Canarian food products on sale in the shop. 📍 Las Cañadas del Teide. ☎ 922 37 48 41 ✉ canadas@parador.es ❶ Credit cards accepted

Restaurant Buffet El Teide ££ Canarian dishes at lunchtime in a pleasant dining room on the Puerto de la Cruz side of the park.
📍 Carretera General TF-21, La Orotava ☎ 922 35 60 35 🕐 Lunch only

Teleférico Picos del Teide Bar £ Snacks, drinks, ice cream and an inexpensive set lunch are served at the lower cable-car station. The bar at the top is closed but the lavatories are open. ☎ 922 69 40 41

The north coast

A popular touring route leads along the north coast past banana plantations and traditional fishing villages, offering dramatic glimpses of the sea beyond green, fertile scenery. Highlights en route are the venerable Dragon Tree in Icod de los Vinos, and the delightful historic town of Garachico.

The twin towns of Los Realejos (Alto and Bajo) both have good restaurants and interesting churches. Icod de los Vinos is a sizeable place spreading up a fertile valley. Founded in the 16th century, it has a most attractive old quarter. Don't miss its charming church and tree-lined central squares surrounded by Canarian-style buildings. As its name suggests, Icod is famous for its wines, which are widely on sale in local *bodegas* and souvenir shops. You'll certainly be invited for a tasting if you go anywhere near the **Dragon Tree (Drago Milenario)**, Icod's main tourist sight, now surrounded by the so-called **Parque Del Drago** (for which there is an entrance fee).

In the hills above the town is a less publicised curiosity, the Cueva del Viento, a huge system of **subterranean lava caves**. Garachico is another well-kept and very interesting seaside town, formerly a major north-coast port rebuilt on an apron of solidified lava after an eruption in 1706 destroyed the earlier town, leaving behind 'El Caleton', a series of natural **seawater pools**. Carefully preserved buildings are dotted around the old quarter, which centres on a shady plaza. The best views are from high above the town, near El Tanque.

Heading further west through the attractive towns of Los Silos and Buenavista, you skirt the northern slopes of the Teno hills. Up in the hills, the typical farming village of El Tanque produces fine wines. Its **17th-century church** and the tourist picnic site of El Lagar may suggest a reason for breaking your journey.

An improved road provides swift access to the Punta de Teno, Tenerife's remote westerly promontory, but signs warn of rockfalls on 'winding [sic] or raining days'. Have your camera ready at the Mirador de Dom Pompeyo. The road ends by the lighthouse with a crash of surf on

⬟ *The dragon tree at Icod de los Vinos*

black rocks. To the south loom the cliffs of Los Gigantes – a good place for picnics (take provisions with you), walks and sunset views.

THINGS TO SEE & DO

Casa de la Cultura

A fine old friary (Convento de San Francisco) on Garachico's main square now houses a folk museum and an exhibition of historic photographs of the town. The building itself is worth a look.

ⓐ Garachico ⓣ 922 83 00 00 ⓛ 10.00–18.00; closed Sun
ⓘ Admission charge

Castillo de San Miguel (Garachico Castle)

A dramatic setting by the harbour enhances this 16th-century fortress which managed to survive the great eruption of 1706. The surrounding lava has been sculpted into rock gardens and swimming pools. Inside is a small museum.

ⓐ Avenida Tome Cano, Garachico ⓣ 922 83 00 01 ⓛ 10.00–18.00
ⓘ Admission charge

Mariposario del Drago (Butterfly Garden)

Tropical wingbeats fan this mini-jungle just round the corner from Icod's Dragon Tree Park. Up to 30 species of butterflies fly free in a 400 sq m (4,300 sq ft) garden. Follow signs to the Drago Milenario.

ⓐ Icod de los Vinos ⓣ 922 81 51 67 ⓦ www.mariposario.com
ⓛ 10.00–18.00 ⓘ Admission charge

TAKING A BREAK

Aristides £ Set on the Plaza Libertad of Garachico this restaurant offers good fresh fish and a peaceful atmosphere. ⓐ Calle Fco Montes de Oca,
ⓣ 922 13 34 12 ⓛ 12.00–17.00 & 18.30–22.00

Casa León £ Inexpensive Canarian cooking and fresh produce is the watchword in this simple, spacious restaurant up in the hills. ⓐ Avenida Villa Nueva 49, La Guancha ⓣ 922 82 80 06 ⓛ 13.00–16.30

El Lagar de Julio £ Local dishes with a dash of innovation – the desserts are particularly good. ⓐ Next to the park Puerta de Tierra, Calle Fco Montes de Oca, Garachico ⓛ 13.30–18.00 & 19.30–23.00 Wed–Sun; closed Mon & Tues.

El Mirador de Garachico £ Snacks and a volcanic view, high above the town. ⓐ Carretera General de Icod a Guia de Isora ⓣ 922 83 02 94 ⓛ 08.00–19.00

Las Piscinas £ One of many popular, good-value taverns in Tenerife's most westerly town specialising in home-cooked fresh fish. ⓐ Calle Molinos 27, Buenavista del Norte ⓣ 922 12 70 33

Piscina Municipal £ The municipal baths may seem an odd choice for a meal, but the Olympic-sized seafront saltwater pool in the pretty town of Los Silos has a good café offering a range of inexpensive fish dishes and Canarian wines. ⓐ El Puertito, Los Silos ⓣ 922 80 00 23

Las Aguas ££ Reliable Spanish cooking in a cosy stone house. Rice and shellfish dishes a speciality. Worth waiting for if there is a queue. ⓐ Calle La Destila 20, San Juan de la Rambla ⓣ 922 36 04 28 ⓛ 13.00–15.30 & 20.00–22.30; closed Sun eve & Mon

El Monasterio ££ A popular tourist restaurant in an ancient monastery dating back to 1646. Spacious grounds with poultry and animals. Delightful, rustic decor and friendly service. Well-prepared Canarian cooking and local wines in a series of rambling dining rooms. ⓐ La Montañeta,12 TF-333, Los Realejos ⓣ 922 34 43 11 ⓛ 09.00–01.00

Northeast of Puerto de la Cruz

Several places are worth exploring in this lush part of the island, though it doesn't usually feature on organised excursion programmes. It's possible to do the main part of the journey by bus, but it's much more convenient to have your own transport.

The *autopista del norte* (northern motorway), signed towards Santa Cruz, provides a swift and painless exit route east of Puerto de la Cruz. If you have more time, and a good navigator, you may like to take the older road which gives better viewpoints. Santa Ursula's **leather factory** is a popular stop-off for visitors. The ominous place-names of La Victoria and La Matanza (meaning 'victory' and 'massacre') and Valle Guerra ('war valley') further north, refer to ancient struggles against the indigenous Guanches, who were finally subdued by the Spaniards at Los Realejos in 1496.

Agua García is a forested region of laurel and heathland. Slip off the motorway at El Sauzal, and follow the coastal route northwards to Punta del Hidalgo, where the road ends by a craggy promontory of the Anaga Hills. It's possible to continue on foot from here to the **troglodytic village of Chinamada** (see page 63).

Flowers and water falls smother the main square of El Sauzal, and a glittering white church makes a photogenic sight, with amazing views of La Palma Island from the church square. Tacoronte is the regional centre of this important wine-producing area, a fairly large Canarian town full of local life in the evenings. Track down two **churches** glittering with New World silver (Santa Catalina and Cristo de los Dolores).

Towards Tejina lies a fertile market-gardening and flower-production region. You may see avocados or papayas growing here, and fields of strelitzias (bird of paradise plants). The older-style holiday developments in this part of Tenerife are mainly used by Germans. Mesa del Mar, near Tacoronte, is a village-like complex of bungalows and apartments around a series of sandy coves. Bajamar is the largest resort, its rocky coast supplemented by two large **seawater bathing pools**.

Punta del Hidalgo, where the road ends, makes a dramatic vantage point, especially at sunset. The distinctive twin rocks, known as the Dos

Hermanos (Two Brothers), rise to over 305 m (1000 ft). Just outside Bajamar, stop off at a German-style roadside café called Melita to indulge in panoramic sea views with afternoon *Kaffee und Kuchen* (coffee and cake).

THINGS TO SEE & DO

Casa del Vino La Baranda

A fascinating museum of wine production, with a showroom for tastings, and an excellent Canarian restaurant and café (see page 61).
ⓐ Casa del Vino, Autopista General del Norte, El Sauzal ❶ 922 57 25 35
ⓦ www.cabtfe.es/casa-vino ● Closed Mon and during May

Museo de Antropología de Tenerife

This charming little museum is housed in a restored 18th-century country house just outside Valle de Guerra. It has interesting displays of Canarian handicrafts and tools, and focuses on the history of food production on Tenerife.
ⓐ Casa de Carta, Valle de Guerra ❶ 922 54 63 00
ⓦ www.museosdetenerife.org ● 09.00–19.00; closed Mon
❶ Admission charge (free on Sun)

TAKING A BREAK

If you have your own transport, explore some of the excellent restaurants near the northern highway. These are patronised by Canarian families at weekends, for whom a day out always involves a very long lunch.

Bajamar £ There's a good selection of snacks and vegetarian food at this attractive terraced beachside restaurant-bar. ⓐ Corner of Avenida Gran Poder/Calle Sin Salida, Bajamar ❶ 922 54 20 52 ● 12.00–22.00

◆ *A colourful sunset near Puerto de la Cruz*

Cofradía de Pescadores £ The restaurant of the guild of fishermen – they serve what they catch. Excellent value for money. ⓐ Punta del Hildalgo ⓘ 922 15 69 54 ⓛ 12.30–23.00; closed Mon

La Tasquita de Carol £ A small and cosy restaurant serving meat and fish in the owner's garden. ⓐ Carretera General 806, Valle de Guerra ⓘ 922 54 40 50 ⓛ 12.30–16.00 & 19.00–23.00 Tues–Sat; closed Mon & Sun eve

Bodega Casa Antonio ££ A popular restaurant-bar just off the motorway offering Canarian and international cooking and local wines. Try fresh tuna rissoles. ⓐ Carretera General del Norte 69, Santa Ursula ⓘ 922 30 06 06 ⓛ Closed Tues

Casa del Vino ££ Taste some of the island's best wines along with good, local cooking in a restored 17th-century building. Full meals or tapas available. ⓐ Autopista General del Norte, El Sauzal ⓘ 922 53 38 86 ⓛ Closed Sun eve, Mon & May

Casa Juan ££ A child-friendly, German-style restaurant with rustic decor and smoked specialities. Home-made sausage and vegetarian dishes, and local Canarian wines. ⓐ Camino de Acentejo 77, La Matanza ⓘ 922 57 70 12 ⓛ 12.30–16.00 & 18.30–22.30; closed Mon & Sun

La Ermita ££ A peaceful, attractive setting of wood makes a backdrop for international seafood and local wines served from the barrel. ⓐ Urbanización Los Angeles 74, El Sauzal ⓘ 922 57 51 74 ⓛ 13.00–16.30 & 19.30–23.30; closed Wed & Sun eve

◯ *La Orotava's picturesque skyline*

La Orotava

This is a delightful old town, which is one of the most popular and accessible excursion destinations from Puerto de la Cruz. La Orotava is also the regional centre of the temperate and fertile valley which bears its name. Once part of the richest of the ancient Guanche kingdoms, it has now expanded from its historic core, spilling down the green slopes towards the former fishing village that is still its coastal trading outlet – Puerto de la Cruz.

The old town is almost miraculously well preserved, and in its steep central streets and squares visitors can enjoy its fine churches and beautiful mansions, notably the elaborate wooden balconies that are such a photogenic feature of the islands. Several of the best houses are now tourist attractions containing handicraft shops and museums.

If you're in La Orotava in late May or early June then don't miss the Corpus Christi Festival when the square in front of the Palacio Municipal is decorated with carpets of flower petals and volcanic sands depicting religious scenes.

THINGS TO SEE & DO

La Casa de los Balcones

An outstanding attraction for visitors, combining one of La Orotava's most striking 17th-century buildings with a chance to watch traditional embroidery and lace demonstrations, buy handicrafts, and visit a small folk museum. See also the similar Casa del Turista opposite.

ⓐ Calle San Francisco 3 ⓣ 922 33 06 29 ⓦ www.casa-balcones.com
ⓛ 10.00–17.00 ⓘ Admission charge to museum; showroom and lower courtyard free

Hijuela del Botánic

This small but exquisite park is crammed with rare palms and exotic plants.

ⓐ Calle Hermano Apolinar ⓣ 922 33 00 50

Hospital de la Santísima Trinidad

Fine views of the Orotava valley can be had from the terrace of this 18th-century Franciscan convent. Notice the revolving wooden drum fixed on the inner door – an anonymous 'letterbox' for foundling babies.
ⓐ Calle San Francisco

Iglesia de Nuestra Señora de la Concepción

La Orotava's most impressive church is an 18th-century baroque replacement of an earlier version destroyed in earthquakes.
ⓐ Plaza Casañas

Museo de Artesanía Iberoamericana

A large collection of South American handicrafts are displayed here in a converted monastery. ⓐ Calle Tomás Zerolo 34 ① 922 35 29 06
🕒 09.30–18.00 Mon–Fri, 09.30–14.00 Sat ❶ Admission charge

Museo de Cerámica

Studio workshop in a 17th-century Canarian house, with pottery on sale.
ⓐ Casa Tafuriaste, Las Candias, on the south-west edge of town
① 922 33 33 96 🕒 10.00–18.00; closed Sun

Oasis del Valle

A family day out with exotic gardens, camel and pony rides, assorted wildlife and a Canarian restaurant.
ⓐ Calle Trasera Camino Torreón 2 ① 922 33 35 09 🕒 10.00–17.00
ⓦ www.oasisdelvalle.com ❶ Admission charge; free bus

TAKING A BREAK

Bar-Restaurante La Duquesa £ A great find for a lunch of authentic Canarian cooking at low prices, served in a relaxed bar popular with locals. ⓐ Plaza Patricio Garcia 6-B ① 922 33 49 49 🕒 07.00–16.00 Mon–Fri

⬥ *A cobbled street in La Orotava*

El Calderito de la Abuela ££ Long-established Canarian restaurant overlooking the Orotava valley. ⓐ Carretera General del Norte 130, Cuesta de la Villa, Santa Ursula ⓣ 922 30 19 18 ⓛ 13.00–16.00 & 19.00–23.00; closed Mon

Casa Lercaro ££ Entering this beautiful restored building is like going back in time – it serves well presented, traditional Canarian food for a decent price. ⓐ Calle Colegio 7, Orotava ⓛ 12.30–16.30 & 20.00–23.00; Sun lunch only

Sabor Canario ££ A charming Canarian restaurant in the fine old mansion containing the Pueblo Guanche folk museum. Crafts and food products on sale. ⓐ Calle Carrera 17 ⓣ 922 32 27 93 ⓛ 12.00–16.00 & 19.30–21.30; closed Sun

La Laguna

The Conquistador Alonso Fernández de Lugo established his headquarters here in 1496 after defeating the Guanches. San Cristobál de la Laguna remained Tenerife's capital until 1723, when it was superseded by Santa Cruz. It is still an important place, as it is the seat of the Canary Islands' only university and also the home of the bishopric of Santa Cruz.

Set on a high plateau in an ancient *laguna* (lake-bed), its modern suburbs now sprawl far beyond its original confines, giving a rather off-putting impression to passers-by on the motorway. Though only about half the size of its near neighbour, Santa Cruz, it is a bewildering place for the motorist. Visitors come here mostly on day trips to visit the museums and explore its delightful old quarter. It has no especially compelling sights but its relaxed Spanish charm is seductive. Student activity keeps it awake – La Laguna is the place to find a decent concert, or an art exhibition.

La Laguna isn't really a tourist town, and, if you visit it, you must expect Spanish ways. Sights and shops close for the siesta period, though that can be a peaceful time to wander round the streets. Sunday morning is a good time to visit – museums are free then and you may find it easier to park.

The main monuments lie in the grid-like streets between the **Iglesia de Nuestra Señora la Concepción** and the **Plaza del Adelantado**. Find a parking spot somewhere in this area. If you walk up **Calle Obispo Rey Redondo** and back down **San Agustín**, you'll see quite a few of La Laguna's main buildings, and can get a flavour of the town in a couple of hours. Its shady plazas, inner courtyards and the dignified facades of handsome colonial buildings give it a memorable atmosphere. The new university campus lies to the south, beside the motorway.

THINGS TO SEE & DO

Catedral de Nuestra Señora de los Remedios

Founded in 1515, the building was remodelled at the beginning of this century in a neo-classical style. Its white and grey exterior is shaded by

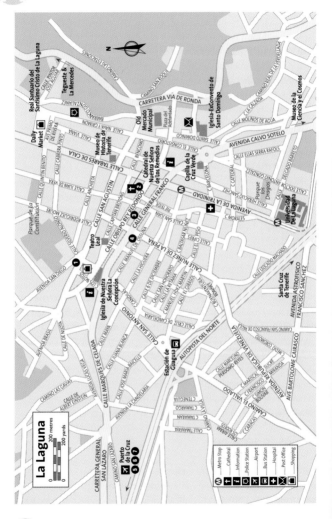

La Laguna

| | 0 | 200 metres |
| | 0 | 200 yards |

Legend:
- Ⓜ Metro Stop
- ⛪ Cathedral
- ℹ Information
- 🚔 Police Station
- ✈ Airport
- 🚌 Bus Station
- ✚ Hospital
- ✉ Post Office
- 🛍 Shopping

slender palms, and inside are some significant works of art. The tomb of Tenerife's first governor, Alonso Fernández de Lugo, lies behind the altar.
ⓐ Calle Obispo Rey Redondo

Iglesia de Nuestra Señora de la Concepción

One of Tenerife's most important churches (1502), its main glories include a magnificent 16th-century coffered ceiling and a cedarwood pulpit. Notice the silver altarpiece, and the ceramic font in which defeated Guanche chieftains were baptised. ⓐ Calle Obispo Rey Redondo

Museo de la Ciencia y el Cosmos

Somewhere to amuse the children on a wet day. There are lots of interactive displays about life, the universe and everything, plus a planetarium. To find it, look out for the radar equipment near the university.
ⓐ Calle Vía Lactea ⓣ 922 31 52 65 ⓛ 09.00–19.00 Tues–Sun
ⓘ Admission charge; free on Sun

Museo de Historia de Tenerife

An entertaining and informative account of the island's history from colonial times, in a fine Canarian house, the Casa Lercaro. Its treasures include some of the earliest known maps of the Canary Islands.
ⓐ Calle San Agustín 22 ⓣ 922 82 59 49 ⓛ 10.00–19.00 Tues–Sun
ⓘ Admission charge; free on Sun

Plaza del Adelantado

This laurel-shaded plaza is typically Canarian. It's a marvellous place to watch the world go by. All around its edges stand imposing historic monuments in Spanish colonial style. Nearby are the covered market and the church of Santo Domingo built in the ornate style known as plateresque.

TAKING A BREAK

La Laguna's eating places reflect a wide range of budgets, from wealthy business folk to impecunious university students. They are rather scattered,

however, and the historic quarter is short on interesting restaurants. You will find more choice on the exit roads to Tacoronte or La Esperanza. Wherever you choose, you can expect an authentic local ambience.

Cafetería San Agustin £ ❶ Nice little café serving coffees, teas and snacks. ⓐ Plaza de la Junta Suprema 2

Ostería de Andreas £ ❷ A small but tastefully done restaurant with a set menu from Wed–Fri: Sunday is pizza day. They also have a good selection of Spanish wines. ⓐ Close to the Cathedral, Calle Deán Palahi 24 ☎ 922 26 05 01 ⏰ 13.30–23.00; closed Mon, Tues & Sun eve

Pizzeria La Carrera £ ❸ Popular with the locals, this restaurant specialises in pizza and pasta dishes but they also do good local meat and fish dishes. ⓐ Calle Obispo Rey Redondo ☎ 922 25 87 41 ⏰ 09.00–23.00

Restaurante Maquila £ ❹ This popular, late-19th-century restaurant stands in the university quarter. Good Canarian wines and typical regional cooking. ⓐ Calle Herradores, La Laguna ☎ 922 25 74 14

El Campo ££ ❺ Grills and sausages served in a country atmosphere of rough-sawn wood and stone. ⓐ Carretera General del Norte 350, Los Naranjeros ☎ 922 56 17 61 ⏰ 13.00–24.00; closed Sun & all of Sept

La Hoya del Camello ££ ❻ Cheerful country-style restaurant, popular with families at weekends. ⓐ Carretera General del Norte 128, La Laguna ☎ 922 26 20 54 ⏰ 11.30–16.30 & 20.00–23.30; closed Mon & Sun eve

Los Limoneros £££ ❼ Smart, long-established, rural restaurant by the golf course, with Spanish meat and fish specialities. Good Riojan wines. ⓐ Carretera General del Norte 447B, Los Naranjeros ☎ 922 63 61 44 ⏰ 13.00–22.30; closed Sun

Santa Cruz de Tenerife

Tenerife's capital lies on a sloping apron of land between a sheltered bay and the steep Anaga Mountains, which shield it from damp trade winds. Tourists visit it mainly for shopping expeditions, or for its astonishing Lent Carnival (usually February), but there's a lot more to it than that.

Most of the main sights lie in the streets immediately behind the Plaza de España. The whole area has been pedestrianised recently. The best city-centre shops are concentrated around Plaza de la Candelaria and Calle de Castillo. El Corte Inglés on Avenida del Tres de Mayo is the biggest department store; you'll also find masses of 'duty-free' outlets.

BEACHES

If you visit Santa Cruz, don't forget your swimming togs. Within the city, the **Parque Marítimo César Manrique** offers a lido complex of landscaped pools similar to the one in Puerto de la Cruz.
ⓐ Avenida La Constitución ⏰ 10.00–18.00 (19.00 in summer)

At **San Andrés**, 6 km (4 miles) north of Santa Cruz, lies Tenerife's most beautiful beach, which the Santacruceros very sensibly keep for themselves rather than exploit for tourists. **Las Teresitas** is a long belt of imported Saharan sand, exquisitely shaded by palms, so far with not a single hotel in sight!

THINGS TO SEE & DO

Centro de Fotografía Isla de Tenerife (Tenerife Photographic Centre)

Just next to the Guimera theatre this absorbing collection of black-and-white and colour photographs takes you on a journey of Tenerife's past right up to the present day.
ⓐ Plaza Isla de la Madera ☎ 922 29 07 35 ⏰ 11.00–13.00, 18.00–21.00; closed Sun

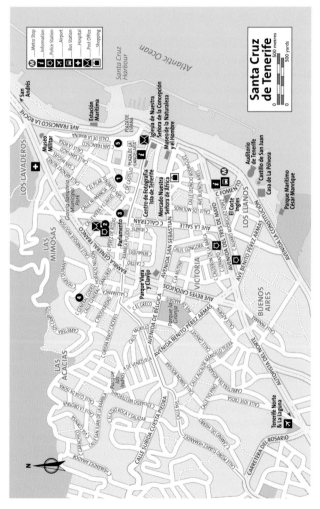

Santa Cruz de Tenerife

Legend:
- Ⓜ Metro Stop
- ℹ Information
- 🚓 Police Station
- ✈ Airport
- 🚌 Bus Station
- ✚ Hospital
- ✉ Post Office
- 🛍 Shopping

Atlantic Ocean

Santa Cruz Harbour

San Andrés

Estación Marítima

Iglesia de Nuestra Señora de la Concepción

Museo de la Naturaleza y el Hombre

Centro de Fotografía Isla de Tenerife

Mercado Nuestra Señora de África

Parlamento

Parque Viera y Clavijo

Auditorio de Tenerife

Castillo de San Juan

Casa de La Pólvora

Parque Marítimo César Manrique

El Corte Inglés

Museo Militar

García Sanabria Municipal Park

Rambla General Franco

Tenerife Norte & La Laguna

0   500 metres
0   500 yards

García Sanabria Municipal Park

Flame trees may blaze, but otherwise all is shade and coolness in this beautiful park dating from the 1920s. Unwind at one of the cafés, listen to the birds, and admire the Miró and Henry Moore sculptures.

ⓐ Off the Rambla del General Franco ❶ Admission free

Iglesia de Nuestra Señora de la Concepción

The distinctive bell tower of Santa Cruz's most important church makes a prominent landmark near the Plaza de España. Dating from 1502, it is one of Tenerife's oldest.

ⓐ Plaza de la Iglesia, Avenida Bravo Murillo

🔺 Shopping in Santa Cruz

◯ *An aerial view of Santa Cruz*

Mercado Nuestra Señora de África

This picturesque produce market is held in a peach-walled enclosure reminiscent of some North African souk. Over 300 stalls display a daily cornucopia of fruits, flowers and spices. On Sunday mornings a lively *rastro* (flea market) is held nearby.

ⓐ South end of Puente Serrador 🕒 06.00–15.00

Museo Militar

Housed in the Cuartel de Almeida (military headquarters) of Paso Alto, the main interest of this small collection of weaponry for British visitors is *El Tigre* (The Tiger), the cannon which allegedly shot off Lord Nelson's arm during a raid on the city in 1797.

ⓐ Calle San Isidro 2 ☎ 922 84 35 00 🕒 10.00–14.00; closed Sun & Mon ❗ Identification required. Admission free

Museo de la Naturaleza y el Hombre

Tenerife's main archaeological and natural history collections are now housed together in fine new premises in the old civil hospital. Good displays on Guanche culture and some fearsomely trepanned skulls.

ⓐ Calle Fuentes Morales ☎ 922 53 58 16 🕒 09.00–19.00 Tues–Sat, 10.00–14.00 Sun ❗ Admission charge; free on Sun

Santa Cruz harbour

Anyone who enjoys messing about in boats will love Santa Cruz. The activity stretches several kilometres up the coast from Plaza de España. Tenerife's tour guides often recite the anecdote that Robert Maxwell met his mysterious fate sailing somewhere off Santa Cruz.

TAKING A BREAK

El Águila ££ ❶ Good coffee or tea with huge slices of superb cake or pastry, they also make sandwiches and bocadillos. Set in a nice little square. ⓐ Alférez Provisional ☎ 922 27 31 56 🕒 09.00–23.00

La Cazuela ££ ❷ A popular café offering excellent tapas and good stews or steaks. ⓐ Robayna ☏ 34 922 27 23 00 🕐 13.30–16.00 & 20.30–24.00; closed Sun

Condal y Peñamil ££ ❸ Good international food in a restaurant which used to be a cigar workshop – part of the restaurant is a small tobacco museum. ⓐ Callejon del Combate 9 ☏ 922 24 49 76 🕐 13.00–16.00 & 20.00–23.00; closed Sun

El Coto de Antonio ££ ❹ A simple but reliable favourite, serving superb regional specialities near the bullring. For a flavour of the local cuisine, try black potato salad or *vieja* (sun fish) in coriander. ⓐ Calle General Goded 13 ☏ 922 27 21 05 🕐 13.00–16.00 & 20.00–24.00; closed Sun eve & Sept

Mesón Los Monjes ££ ❺ A highly regarded Basque restaurant in smart wood-panelled surroundings. Fish and sausage are specialities. ⓐ Calle de la Marina 17 ☏ 922 24 65 76 🕐 Closed Sun

Candelaria, Las Caletillas & the east coast

Candelaria is the main focus of attention along this coast, attracting visitors and pilgrims to the Basílica de Nuestra Señora de Candelaria and its much-venerated statue. Just to the north lies Las Caletillas, an understated resort of apartment blocks by small beaches of dark sand.

The bleached coastal strip of eastern Tenerife lacks many attractions in terms of scenery. There are a few small resorts, but nothing like the huge developments elsewhere. Most tourists see it from the *autopista del sur* (motorway of the south) which runs from Playa de las Américas to the north of the island. This is a speedy and convenient way of getting between Santa Cruz and the major resorts or to and from the airports, but it's a fairly boring journey. If you have more time to explore, take the older inland route through Arico, Fasnia and Güímar. There are no unmissable points of interest along the way, but you pass through genuine Canarian villages and much more attractive scenery. The TF-28 is a sunny, flower-decked corniche trickling through orchards and vineyards beneath ancient volcano craters. If you find the winding inland route too time-consuming, simply rejoin the motorway via any of half a dozen linking roads which were originally constructed to provide access from the hill settlements to the little coastal ports.

THINGS TO SEE & DO

Arafo

This neat whitewashed village, inland from Candelaria, is surrounded by orchards, flowers and vineyards. Behind it looms an old volcano, the Montaña de las Arenas, which erupted destructively in 1705–6. Arafo is noted for its cultural traditions, especially its folk music, and a popular *romería* (pilgrimage) at the end of August. The church contains some fine wooden sculptures.

◔ Statue of a Guanche king along Candelaria's seafront

Arico Viejo

This pretty little hill village is the centre of a fertile agricultural zone growing tomatoes and potatoes in terraced fields. The church dates from the 17th century. The port of Arico is the fishing village of Poris de Abona, now a small resort. There's an attractive low-rise German holiday village here, and some limited swimming facilities.

Candelaria

The large modern basilica (1959), by the sea, houses a revered image of the island's patron, the Virgin, bright with silver, candles and bouquets of flowers (🕐 07.30–13.00 and 15.00–19.30). Car access to the basilica is banned, so park by the harbour and stroll a short distance up the main street to the large paved square. Notice the bronze statues of Guanche kings along the seafront. There are several stretches of dark sand near the town, mostly used by locals. The older parish church of Santa Ana dates from the 18th century and contains a fine crucifix.

Fasnia

The volcanic landscapes around this little place have been painstakingly cultivated into vineyards and orchards, but the town was spared from disaster when the nearby volcanoes erupted in the early 18th century. There are good coastal views from the white Chapel of Nuestra Señora de los Dolores (Our Lady of the Sorrows), which was built in gratitude.

Guïmar

This rich plateau lies on a geological fault-line below a volcano. The town has a couple of interesting churches and a little museum. Its oddest sights are the Pyramids of Guïmar (🕐 09.30–18.00), a mysterious collection of stone structures which Thor Heyerdahl, the Norwegian explorer, identified as ancient Guanche cult-sites. There is clear evidence of Guanche settlements in the caves of Guïmar, but the visitor centre's interpretation of these finds is controversial. The Mirador de Don Martin, above the town, offers marvellous views. A small resort has developed around the fishing port of Puerto de Guïmar.

TAKING A BREAK

Simple, typical Canarian restaurants and bars can be found in many of the hill villages and their ports. Try the local wines, which can be very good.

Rincón de Tara £ You find this little restaurant in an old house next to the Church of San Pedro. Has a good variety of dishes. ⓐ Imeldo Serís 2, Güimar ⓣ 922 51 42 27 ⓛ 13.00–16.30 & 20.00–23.30; closed Mon & Sun eve

La Rueda £ Delightful little tapas bar serving a selection of alcoholic and soft drinks. ⓐ Avenida del Generalisimo, Las Caletillas, opposite Tenerife Tour Hotel ⓣ 922 50 12 63 ⓛ 13.00–16.00 & 20.00–23.00; closed Wed

Casa Manolo II ££ Fresh fish and local wines in no-frills surroundings. ⓐ Avenida del Cabildo 9 ⓣ 922 70 61 30 ⓛ 12.00–17.00 & 19.00–22.30; closed Mon, lunch only Sun

Frontos ££ Seasonal food in a rural setting. The gazpacho with avocado and toasted ham and the cod with sweet potato and saffron sauce are highly recommended. ⓐ Lomo Grande 3, Los Blanquitos (TF-28 km 70,2), Granadilla de Abono ⓣ 922 77 72 54 ⓛ 13.00–16.00 & 19.00–22.30; closed Mon & Tues, Sun lunch only

El Rey de la Gamba ££ In a little street off the Plaza, this restaurant serves good fish, shellfish and paellas in a pleasant, relaxed atmosphere. ⓐ Obispo Perez Caceres 10, Candelaria ⓣ 922 50 63 76 ⓛ 12.00–16.00 & 20.00–24.00

El Archete £££ Acclaimed and ambitious Canarian cuisine in a fine old timber-framed house. Smart surroundings. ⓐ Lomo de Aroba 2, Candelaria ⓣ 922 50 03 54 ⓛ 13.00–17.00 & 20.00–24.00; closed Sun & at Easter

The south coast

Most visitors get a fleeting glimpse of this arid part of the island as they land or take off from Tenerife's international airport. The area is generally known as the Costa del Silencio (Coast of Silence), which may seem a bit of a joke considering how close it is to the runway. The coastal scenery looks immensely bleak and desert-like, but it's a productive agricultural zone, with bananas and vines sheltering from the wind in cages of plastic netting or breeze-block compounds, and irrigated by giant underground reservoirs.

A number of small resorts have developed along the low, rocky coastline, and are becoming more popular with British visitors. The large bungalow complexes of Belgian-owned Ten-Bel, or neighbouring El Chapparal, are typical holiday villages near the fishing port of **Las Galletas**. Not much happens at night, but sports facilities are good and there are a number of tourist attractions just off the motorway (some of these are listed in the section on Los Cristianos on pages 14–17).

El Médano is a small town with some resort facilities and two sizeable stretches of sand dominated by the hook-nosed **Montaña Roja** (Red Mountain), the cinder-cone of an ancient volcano. Unusual drought-loving plants grow in the inhospitable Saharan landscapes. International windsurfing championships are held here. A local wind-farm also takes advantage of the prevailing *alisios* (north-east trade winds), providing energy to over 3,000 homes.

A ten-minute drive inland will take you into another world of traditional island villages. The higher into the hills you go, the prettier and more fertile the scenery. **Granadilla de Abona** is the regional centre, a modest hill town in a prosperous farming area. From here, attractive drives lead through San Miguel and Valle de San Lorenzo, where you can get a good idea of the terrain from the **Mirador de la Centinela**.

Heading up towards **Vilaflor**, you traverse one of the most appealing approaches to **Mount Teide**. One of the most remarkable sights in the district is the astonishing **Paisaje Lunar** (lunar landscape), a series of strangely shaped pyramidal rocks, which look just like weathered termite hills, located on the fringes of the national park. They are accessible only on foot.

One of the best things to do in this area is to head to the little fishing village of Los Abrigos for a typical fish lunch. Restaurants line the harbour, so saunter down the hill and check the menus. You may like to make this your last memory of Tenerife before checking in for your return flight. The airport is just ten minutes' drive away.

BEACHES

The coastline west of **El Médano** is low-lying and rocky. Bathing is possible in a few coves via flights of steps running into the sea, but there is no sand, and most visitors to the area use local seawater swimming pools. **Las Galletas** has a small, stony beach mostly used by locals. **El Médano**, however, is one of the rare places on Tenerife with

Playa de las Visitas, Los Cristianos

naturally blonde beaches. Here the prevailing winds carry sand from the Sahara. The long stretches on either side of the **Montaña Roja** are unspoilt and gently shelving but very exposed to the wind, with no natural shade. The smaller beaches of **El Cabezo** and **La Jaquita** further afield are recommended for expert swimmers only.

THINGS TO SEE & DO

Fun and games

Go-karting is available near the airport. The holiday villages entertain their guests with a wide range of activities, including tennis, riding, fishing, diving and sailing. There's a hang-gliding centre in Valle de San Lorenzo. Donkey safaris and camel rides are advertised from Las Galletas. If you want some fun in the evening, you could head for the Castillo San Miguel, where a popular restaurant show takes place nightly on a medieval theme.

Golf

Two 18-hole golf courses, **Amarilla** (**☏** 922 73 03 19) and **Golf del Sur** (**☏** 922 73 81 70 **Ⓦ** www.amarillagolf.es/golfdelsur.es), make unnatural splashes of green on the barren cinders of the Costa del Silencio. There is also a 9-hole golf course, **Los Palos**, on the road between Guaza and Las Galletas (**☏** 922 16 90 80 **Ⓦ** www. golflospalos.com).

Water sports

There are diving centres at Las Galletas and El Médano, but the latter is more famous as a windsurfer's paradise. You can hire sailboards and book tuition here, or simply watch experts zip through the waves at astonishing speeds.

TAKING A BREAK

Mirador la Centinela £ Glass-sided restaurant with a fantastic view of the south coast. Serves coffees and teas as well as a complete menu.

 On the TF-28 (km 85) from Valle San Lorenzo to San Miguel
 922 69 12 84  10.00–23.00; closed Mon

Casa Tagoro ££ Enjoy good food set in the beautiful surroundings of a restored 300-year-old Canarian mansion.  Calle Tagoro 28, Granadilla de Abona  922 77 22 40  18.30–23.30 Tues–Thur, 12.30–23.00 Fri & Sat; closed Sun

El Jable £££ Rustic surroundings of wood and volcanic stone mix with bright modern paintings. Canarian specialities include grilled cheese with coriander sauce. Art exhibitions and wine tastings.  Bentejui 9, San Isidro, Granadilla de Abona  922 39 06 98  13.00–16.00 & 19.30–23.00; closed Mon lunch & Sun

Los Roques £££ Run by an English couple and offering a blend of international flavours. The chef has lived in several countries from France, India, America and all this experience is used in his creations. The Calle La Marina dessert is particularly good.  Los Abrigos  922 74 94 01  19.00–23.00; closed Mon  Book ahead

La Gomera

La Gomera is the second smallest of the Canary Islands, a compact green roundel about 24 km (15 miles) across, just 32 km (20 miles) west of Tenerife. Daily flights connect from Tenerife South airport to Playa de Santiago and it is easily reached by car ferry from Los Cristianos in 45 minutes. A 25-minute fast car hydrofoil also leaves four times a day from Los Cristianos. Longer boat trips, including whale- and dolphin-watching tours, are advertised from Los Gigantes.

San Sebastián, the main town and port, lies on the east coast. Among its boxy white houses are several minor sights associated with Christopher Columbus, who made La Gomera his last port of call before those daring voyages to the New World. To the south lies Playa de Santiago, a growing resort amid arid hills. The west coast hides fertile Shangri-La valleys and Nile-like vegetation. The lovely northern villages of Agulo, Hermigua and Vallehermoso glow with brilliant creepers and fruit trees. Coastal tracks lead down to unspoilt pebbly beaches, and rock formations, such as **El Roque Cano** (the Dog Rock) or **La Fortaleza** (the Castle), make striking landmarks.

The most spectacular scenery, however, lies in the centre of the island. The mountainous **Garajonay National Park** is classified as a Unesco World Heritage Site for its primeval laurel forests – a haven for rare subtropical species where damp rock-faces sprout ferns and mosses, and lichens trail like cobwebs from the trees. Excursion parties tour the island by coach, often stopping at a craft centre and a popular restaurant for lunch and a demonstration of La Gomera's ancient whistling language – called *silbo* – by which means the islanders used to send messages across steep valleys.

THINGS TO SEE & DO

Casa de la Aguada

In San Sebastián's old Custom House you'll find Columbus's well, from which he replenished his ships' water tanks. A plaque is inscribed with

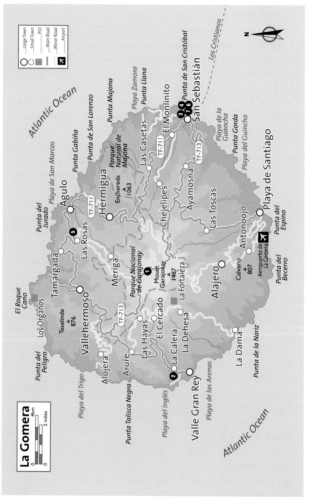

the words: 'With this water, America was baptised'. The new visitor centre gives more information.

🅐 Calle Real 4, San Sebastián 🕾 922 87 02 81

El Cercado

Various local workshops in this village produce a type of native pottery called *Chipude* ware, traditionally made without a wheel.

Iglesia de la Asunción

Legend has it that Columbus prayed in this little church before his voyage. Most of the present building, however, was rebuilt after a fire in 1618.

🅐 San Sebastián

Juego de Bolas Visitor Centre

A good place to learn a little about island life, with a handicraft museum and an exhibition about the Garajonay National Park.

🅐 Las Rosas 🕒 09.30–16.30 Tues–Sun

Los Organos

These curious basalt columns, along a stretch of cliffs, can be reached by boat from Puerto Vallehermoso, on the north coast.

Parque Nacional de Garajonay

Not to be missed, even if you haven't got a clue about plants or birds. The scenery is marvellous, though try to go there on a clear day.

Valle Gran Rey

The staircase terraces and palm trees of this fertile westerly region are some of the most beautiful and spectacular landscapes on the island. It's popular with New Age settlers seeking greener lifestyles.

If La Gomera gives you a taste for seeing the other little islands of the western archipelago, consider visiting La Palma and El Hierro, it's quite

◆ *The La Gomeran town of Agulo, with Mount Teide behind*

easy to reach them by plane from Tenerife, allowing you enough time to get a good idea of the islands by rental car or taxi. A few excursion companies offer them as day trips, but you can go independently. It isn't practical to take the slow ferries from Los Cristianos just for a day.

TAKING A BREAK

La Laguna Grande £ ❶ A useful place to stoke up and enjoy the views of the National Park. ⓐ Parque Nacional de Garajonay 🕒 12.00–18.00; closed Mon

Mirador La Calera £ ❷ Just a bit further along the coast from Valley Gran Rey but well worth the journey for the stunning view. Specialises in meat dishes and paellas. ☎ 922 80 50 86 🕒 13.00–17.00 & 18.00–22.30; closed Thur

La Tasca £ ❸ This popular, inexpensive restaurant, occupying a historic house, offers a wide range of dishes from down-to-earth favourites to Canarian classics to imaginative international cooking. ⓐ Calle Ruiz de Padrón 54, San Sebastian ☎ 922 14 15 98 🕒 13.00–15.30 & 19.00–23.00

Casa del Mar ££ ❹ A big choice of fish and seafood dishes is on the menu at this bright, popular restaurant located near the seafront. ⓐ Paseo Fred Olsen 2, San Sebastián ☎ 922 87 03 20 🕒 11.00–16.00 & 17.00–23.00; closed Tues ❗ Credit cards accepted

Parador de San Sebastián de la Gomera ££ ❺ This lovely old hotel, high above the town, has elegant surroundings, gorgeous gardens and unparalleled views. Typical, Gomeran cooking (full meals or snacks). ⓐ Cerro de la Orca, Balcón de la Villa y Puerto, San Sebastián ☎ 922 87 11 00 🕒 13.30–15.30 & 19.30–22.30

Las Rosas ££ ❻ This popular tourist lunch stop is noted for its good views and demonstrations of the silbo whistling language. ⓐ Las Rosas ❶ 922 80 09 16 🕐 12.00–15.00

Marquès de Oristano £££ ❼ One of the best places for a top-quality meal is conveniently placed for the inter-island ferry. Enjoy a relaxed style and fine dining on the outdoor terrace. ⓐ Calle del Medio, San Sebastián ❶ 922 87 29 01 🕐 All day

▶ *Fishing boats in the harbour at Los Cristianos*

🔺 *Vine tending in the wine valleys of Orotava*

Food & drink

New arrivals in Playa de las Américas may be puzzled, and perhaps a bit disheartened, to find signs proudly announcing 'No Spanish food here' or 'Genuine British Breakfasts' in some popular tourist areas. Don't despair if your idea of a holiday abroad involves more adventurous eating. There are lots of good restaurants throughout the island happy to serve a taste of real Canarian food. Local cooking is basically Spanish, of course, with many of the classic dishes of the mainland (paella, gazpacho, calamares, etc) as well as home-grown specialities, spiked with unusual hot and salty flavours, and perhaps the tropical sweetness of bananas.

A TASTE OF THE SEA

The Canary Islands stand in some of the world's richest fishing grounds. The currents that wash the west African coast teem with an astonishing cornucopia of seafood, though the indiscriminate hoovering of breeding shoals by scores of international trawlers is sadly taking its toll. Fish prices are steadily rising and the choice of rarer species diminishing. Local menus still offer plenty of fishy dishes, although beware of fish priced by the kilo rather than the portion – the bill may be heftier than you think. King of Canarian fish is the *vieja* (sun fish). Others are *cherne* (bass), *mero* (perch), *atún* (tuna) and *bacalao* (cod). The delicate flavours of many Canarian white fish are best enjoyed after plain cooking, but fish soups and stews – *sancocho* or *cazuela* – are popular too. And of course, there's plenty of fish and chips!

TRADITIONAL CANARIAN STYLE

Restaurants described as *típico* generally offer a chance to try regional cooking, often in pleasant, rustic surroundings. Canarian cuisine doesn't scale any great gastronomic heights, but it is always unpretentious and fresh local produce makes it very appetising. Look out for traditional Canarian dishes such as *conejo en salmorejo* (rabbit in a spicy sauce), or *ropa vieja* (a classic beef or minced meat stew). Typical accompaniments include *papas arrugadas* (small jacket potatoes cooked in salt) and dips called *mojo*. There are two kinds of *mojo*: a fiery red type based on peppers and chilli called *rojo picante*, and a less piquant green sauce based on parsley and coriander called *mojo rojo suave*.

Another local curiosity is *gofio*, or toasted cereal meal, which has been eaten in the Canaries since prehistoric times. If you want to try it, look out for *escaldón* (seasoned broth with *gofio*). Vegetables are varied and of excellent quality; you'll see them freshly piled up in all the markets. *Puchero canario* is a vegetable hot-pot. If you order a salad, it is generally served as a starter.

PUDDINGS

Canarian puddings tend to be very sweet, often containing almonds or honey. *Bienmesabe* (pronounced 'bee-en-me-saab-ee', the Spanish for 'This tastes really good!') is a typical concoction. You can buy little pots of it ready packed to take home.

🔺 *Bananas are the main ingredient in* Cobana, *the local spirit*

WINES

Tenerife's wines have come a long way in recent years and production is now carefully controlled. The best vintages (red, white and rosé) are well worth drinking; unfortunately some restaurants still serve up bright pink vinegar as *vino del país*, in the belief that tourists know no better.

To sample some decent stuff, head for a reliable *bodega* or join an excursion to the Casa del Vino in El Sauzal (a renowned wine region in the north), which does a good job of promoting the island's wines and has an excellent traditional Canarian restaurant.

In the 16th century Tenerife wines were made with a type of grape known as the sweet Malvasia grape (Canary Sack was Falstaff's favourite tipple) but now they are produced in a range of classic European styles. Prices, however, tend to be fairly high because the scale of commercial production is small.

Other drinks

Ron (rum) is distilled in the Canaries, and often mixed with cola to make the classic hispanic cocktail called a *cuba libre*. A sweeter local drink is *ronmiel*, which is a liqueur made from palm sap extracted in the neighbouring island of La Gomera. *Cobana* is a sticky yellow brew made from bananas – an acquired taste; so worth trying before you buy a whole bottle which may clog up your drinks cabinet for a decade or two. *Sangría* is widely promoted for tourists – few locals touch it. Dorada and Reina are local brands of bottled lager; ask for a *caña* if you want a glass of draught beer.

YES, WE HAVE LOTS OF BANANAS

This crop took off commercially in the late 19th century. The 'dwarf cavendish' does best, a small, curved variety. It adapts well to local conditions, but it hates the wind, so it is often grown behind breeze-block walls. You'll see the lush plantations in many parts of the island, especially in the Orotava Valley and around the south coast.

Menu decoder

Aceitunas en mojo Olives in hot sauce
Bocadillo Filled roll
Ensalada Salad
Helado Ice cream
Perrito caliente Hot-dog
Tapas Snack

TYPICAL CANARIAN DISHES

Cabrito Kid (goat)
Chipirones Small squid
Conejo al salmorejo Rabbit in hot chilli sauce
Escaldon de pescado Fish, vegetables and maize meal stew
Gambas ajillo Prawns in garlic sauce
Garbanzasa Chickpea stew with meat
Lomo Slices of pork
Papas arrugadas Small jacket potatoes boiled in very salty water, served with *mojo picante* (hot chilli sauce) or *mojo verde* (herb and garlic sauce)
Pata de cerdo Roast leg of pork

Pechuga empanada Breaded chicken breast or chicken breast in batter
Potage Thick vegetable soup (may contain added meat)
Potage de berros Watercress soup
Puchero Meat and vegetable stew
Queso Cheese
Ranchos Noodles, beef and chickpeas
Ropa vieja Chickpeas, vegetables and potatoes (although meat can be added)
Sancocho Salted fish with potatoes and sweet potatoes

DESSERTS

Arroz con leche Cold rice pudding
Bienmesabe A mix of honey and almonds (delicious poured over ice cream)
Flan Crême caramel
Fruta del tiempo Fresh fruit in season
Truchas Turnovers filled with pumpkin jam

DRINKS

Agua mineral Mineral water **con gas/sin gas** Fizzy/still

Batido Milkshake

Café Coffee

Café con leche Coffee with milk

Café cortado Small white coffee

Café descafeinado Decaffeinated coffee

Café solo Black coffee

Cerveza Beer

Leche Milk

Ron Local rum

Té Tea

Vino Wine

Vino blanco White wine

Vino rosado Rosé wine

Vino tinto Red wine

Zumo de naranja Orange juice

SPECIALITY DRINKS

Bitter kas Similar to Campari but non-alcoholic

Cocktail Atlantico Rum, dry gin, banana liqueur, blue curaçao, pineapple nectar

Cocktail Canario Rum, banana cream liqueur, orange juice, cointreau, a drop of grenadine

Guindilla Rum-based cherry liqueur

Mora Blackberry liqueur

Ronmiel Rum-honey, a local speciality

Sangría Mix of red wine, spirits and fruit juices. Can be made with champagne on request

Shopping

In the main resorts, shops are principally geared towards visitors and often clustered together in giant covered malls (look for the magic words 'Centro Comercial'). Besides the everyday holiday mainstays sold in supermarkets, pharmacies and newsagents, the best buys to take home include leather goods, alcohol, tobacco, jewellery, perfume and electronics. All these can be good value, but you need to check quality and prices carefully to be sure of getting a genuine bargain.

FLOWERS

You won't stay long on Tenerife without spotting the island's exotic emblem, the Bird of Paradise, or *strelitzia*, whose exotic flame and navy flowers emerge in crests of spectacular waxy plumage from beak-like buds. They last for ages in water, and when one flower fades, you'll find another tightly furled in the 'beak', waiting to emerge in pristine glory. It's well worth bringing a pack home with you. Order them a few days before you leave and a robust, air-freight box will be delivered to your hotel. The airlines are well used to handling these flowers, so don't worry about checking them in.

FOOD PRODUCTS

Cheese, honey, *mojo* sauces, dried fruit, nuts, wines and liqueurs are some of the most popular buys. You can find these on produce stalls and in supermarkets, or tourist shops and visitor centres. The *parador* shop in Parque Nacional del Teide has a good range of edible goodies, including chocolate almond sweets called *piedras del Teide* (Teide Stones). For wines, check the Casa del Vino in El Sauzal, where you can taste before you buy, and collect your purchases in a handy carrying pack.

MARKETS

Large flea markets are held regularly in several resort venues on Tenerife.

- Torviscas market, in Playa de las Américas, takes place on Thursdays and Saturdays. 🕘 09.00–14.00 ℹ️ near Puerto Colón

- Los Cristianos has a Sunday market. ◕ 09.00–14.00 ❶ at the Arona Gran Hotel – south end of the beach
- In Puerto de la Cruz the market is in a new building on Avenida de Blas Pérez González.
- Los Abrigos market takes place on Tuesday. ◕ 18.00–22.00
- Santa Cruz's popular Sunday morning *rastro* is on Avenida Bravo Murillo, next to the charming daily produce market of Nuestra Señora de África.
- In addition, many Canarian towns and villages hold summer handicraft markets once or twice a year. Garachico has one on the first Sunday of every month. Ask the tourist office for a list.

NATURAL FLOWER PERFUMES

Sniff and select from a wide range of scents packed in attractive little bottles. Some fragrances are a little bit cloying, and they need using up fairly quickly.

POTTERY

Ceramics based on traditional Guanche styles (made without a wheel) can be found in some places. Other souvenirs include basketware, dolls, carvings, jewellery, glassware and paintings.

THREADWORK & EMBROIDERY

An easily portable buy is the classic drawn-thread embroidery known as *calados* (made into table or bed linen, blouses, etc). It's sold especially in La Orotava where there is a working embroidery school. *Petit-point* table mats are a popular and affordable buy. Lacework is a speciality of Vilaflor. Genuine handmade products are expensive. Cheap lookalikes sold on the streets are probably machined somewhere in the Far East.

Children

As in all Spanish destinations, children are very welcome, and there's plenty for them to do.

ANIMALS, PARKS & GARDENS
Camel rides
Always a favourite, and available at three centres on the island.
🅐 One is near Los Cristianos, the other is behind Puerto de la Cruz, and the third one is at El Tanque (above Garachico, in the north).
🕒 10.00–18.00

Loro Parque
Perhaps the best day's entertainment anywhere on the island. Besides the parrots and penguins, there are dolphins, sea lions, an aquarium, bats, shows, cafés, gorillas and tigers, a Thai village and an African-style market (see page 45). 🅐 Avenida Loro Parque, Puerto de la Cruz

Parque Las Águilas
This park includes birds of prey, crazy golf and bob-sleigh rides in an exotic landscape of Wild West cacti and tropical jungles. There are also falconry demonstrations (see page 16). 🅐 Los Cristianos

WATER BABIES
Aqualand Costa Adeje
An exciting experience for all (see page 19). 🅐 Costa Adeje

Boat trips
Try a pirate picnic cruise, a trip on a Spanish galleon, or a whale and dolphin safari on a luxury catamaran. Even more exciting is the Yellow Submarine, based in Las Galletas, which makes regular voyages to the bottom of the sea. Some full-day excursions (such as La Gomera) may be a bit too long for young children.

Aqualand, Playa de las Américas

Siam Park

This huge Thai-themed water park promises to be Europe's biggest and most extravagant when it opens in summer 2008. Using state-of-the-art desalination processes, the park's attractions include a huge meandering river, wave pool, head-spinning adrenaline rides and cascading waterfalls.

ACTIVITIES

La Caldera del Rey

Horse riding for beginners or experienced riders on an old working farm in the hills above Playa de las Americas and Los Cristianos. They also provide pedal carts and mini-tractors for those who prefer four wheels to four legs. ⓦ www.tenerifehorses.com

Castillo de San Miguel

Enjoy a lively evening of feasting and fun at this 16th-century fortress, with the chance to watch an exciting jousting tournament (see page 56). ⓐ Avenida Tome Cano Garachico

Go-karting

Take the kids for a spin. ⓐ Near the airport ⓣ 922 73 07 03

Sports & activities

It can sometimes be quite windy in the Canaries, but generally, the mild, sunny climate is very conducive to all sorts of outdoor activities. Sports facilities are widely advertised in all the resorts.

CYCLING
Bikes can be hired from all the major resorts, including sophisticated multi-speed mountain bikes and more sedate family models. Expect to pay around 6–12 euros per day, but shop around for the best prices.

GOLF
Now boasting nine full-sized courses, Tenerife is well equipped in the golf stakes, but greens are often booked solid through the high season so ring ahead. The largest course is the 27-hole championship course of Golf del Sur; oldest and smartest is the Real Club near La Laguna, a typical British institution. In addition there are several smaller courses (eg the 9-hole Golf Los Palos at Las Galletas), and crazy golf too. For information visit Ⓦ www.webtenerife.com or the booking agency Tenerife Golf Services Ⓦ www.tenerifegolf-services.com

SCUBA DIVING
This is a popular activity all round the coast, with multilingual *centros de buceo* (diving centres) in Santa Cruz, Puerto de la Cruz, Los Gigantes, Playa de las Américas, Los Cristianos, Playa Paraiso and the Costa del Silencio. The narrow shelves of volcanic rock around the Canary Islands bank suddenly to great depths, where vast numbers of sea creatures inhabit the cool, clear waters. There are no very dangerous species near the Canaries and sunken wrecks and caves add an extra *frisson* to underwater exploration. Night dives and photography expeditions can be organised in some places.

TENNIS
The main resorts offer a handful of public tennis courts, but most are based in hotels or apartment complexes. These may be hired by

non-residents. Coaching in squash and tennis is offered at **Tenisur**, Playa de las Américas. Tournaments are held on Wednesdays at the Hotel Las Palmeras, Playa de las Américas (☎ 922 79 09 91). There is also a tennis and paddle club complex, **Las Arenas** (eight lawns in all), near Puerto de la Cruz, which is open at night (☎ 922 37 46 06 ⏰ 09.00–23.30 Mon–Fri, 09.00–20.00 Sat, 09.00–15.00 Sun).

WALKING

Close to Playa de las Américas is a two- to three-hour route through the Barranco del Infierno, a dramatic ravine with a waterfall. Inland, the national park of Las Cañadas offers a fine range of walks at various levels of difficulty. Footpath maps are available from any tourist office. Free guided walks depart daily except Sunday from the park visitor centre (☎ 922 29 01 29).

WATER PARKS

In Puerto de la Cruz, try the Lido (**Lago de Martiánez**). For a modest entrance charge, you can use its facilities all day – sunbeds, parasols, showers, cafés, etc – within earshot of real, crashing surf. At Playa de las Américas, the wild watery rides of the **Aqualand Costa Adeje** provide endless amusement for children. **Parque Marítimo** in Santa Cruz is a smaller reproduction in the same style as the naturalist-designed Lido in Puerto de la Cruz.

WATER SPORTS

All the main resorts have facilities, but you'll find the widest range on the beach playgrounds of Playa de las Américas and Los Cristianos. The natural beaches of Tenerife consist of black volcanic sand or cinders, but some are artificially replenished at intervals with bleaching doses of Saharan sand.

WINDSURFING

The main centre for this is El Médano on the south-east coast, where world championships are regularly held – exciting to watch on a windy day. Some beaches are best left to the experts, but tuition and equipment are available. You can practise in more sheltered conditions at Santa Cruz's Las Teresitas beach, and at Playa de las Américas (behind Hotel Conquistador).

Festivals & events

CANARIAN FOLK & FLAMENCO

Hovering somewhere between the Old World and the New, Canarian folk music can often be heard in the more typical bars and restaurants of the island, and at fiestas. If it appeals to you, recordings of this style of music are on sale in many tourist shops. The Latin-Spanish dance rhythms are easy on the ear, and the somewhat repetitive melodies are played on a range of instruments including guitars, drums, flutes or the Canarian stringed instrument called the *timple*.

Flamenco music, Moorish in origin, swings from impassioned heights to deep melancholia. Folk and flamenco evenings are regularly staged by hotels, restaurants and nightclubs but are inevitably somewhat touristy.

FESTIVALS

In any Spanish destination there's always something festive happening. Tenerife is no exception, and though many events are designed with an eye towards the tourist trade, these are essentially local celebrations, some with a long history. Visitors are always welcome to join in.

⬤ *A dancer takes a rest at the Santa Cruz Shrovetide Carnival*

Some revolve around the Catholic calendar of saints' days, pilgrimages and religious festivals; other events are simply a good excuse for a party.

Throughout the summer months, *romerías* (country festivals with a religious theme) take place in various locations. The biggest event by far, and a good enough reason to book your holiday around it, is Santa Cruz's huge Shrovetide Carnival, on a scale outshone only by Rio de Janeiro.

AFTER DARK

An outing is the **Castillo de San Miguel**, where a jousting tournament and banquet take place in a medieval setting in the hills behind Reina Sofia airport.

For a spectacular evening, dress up a little and try the Spanish Classical Ballet show in Playa de la Américas (at the **Pirámide de Arona** auditorium, the flamboyantly designed congress centre near the Mediterranean Palace Hotel). The show is a mix of ballet, flamenco, folk and modern dancing staged every night except Monday.

☎ 922 75 75 49 for reservations

Tenerife has three casinos; the newest addition is the Lago de Martiánez casino in Puerto de la Cruz. Commanding views over the north coast and ornamental gardens add to the glamour of the gaming tables. Smart dress, a small admission fee and your passport are required. No photography. The other casinos are in Santa Cruz (**Mencey Hotel**) and in Playa de las Américas (**Hotel Gran Tinerfe**).

If your tastes run to classical music, Tenerife has a fine symphony orchestra which holds seasonal concerts. Santa Cruz stages an opera season and various theatrical productions, while La Laguna has regular exhibitions and a lively mix of cultural entertainment. For more details, look out for advertised shows and check the tourist newspapers.

▶ *A warning sign on the road to Mount Teide*

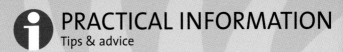

Accommodation

Price ratings are based on a double room for one night.
£ = up to €100   **££** = €100–€150   **£££** = over €150

PLAYA LOS CRISTIANOS
Apartments Los Alisios £ A short walk from the beach, yet set in a quiet part of the resort, these are simple yet spacious apartments, with typical Canarian balconies and pleasant gardens. 🅐 Calle Andorra, vieja carretera a Guaza 📞 922 790 180 🅦 www.coral-hotels.com

Hotel Reverón Plaza £££ Close to the beach and bristling with the latest sporting equipment (and instructors) there's also an aerobic gym and Pilates. The service area includes a sauna, Jacuzzi, Turkish bath, jet shower and there is a heated pool on the roof. All rooms have a balcony and air-conditioning. 🅐 Calle General Franco 26 📞 922 757 120 🅦 www.hotelesreveron.com

PLAYA LAS AMERICAS
Apart-hotel Coral ££ Centrally situated and newly refurbished, this complex is a good choice for families and couples. 🅐 Calle Noelia Afonso 10 📞 922 752 040 🅦 www.coral-hotels.com

Apartments Hacienda del Sol ££ The well laid-out complex is built in the typical Canarian style in midst of a subtropical garden. The studios and apartments are nicely decorated and a short hop from the beach. 🅐 Arquitecto Gómez Cuesta 5 📞 922 791 907 🅦 www.haciendadelsol-tenerife.com

COSTA ADEJE
Apart-hotel El Duque ££ This complex is only 400 m (437 yds) from Fañabé beach and has over 200 well-equipped studios and apartments. With day and night activities and lots of sports facilities. 🅐 Avenida Bruselas 📞 922 718 500 🅦 www.el-duque.com

PLAYA PARAISO, CALLAO SALVAJE, LA CALETA

Apartments Albatros £ These apartments include all the basics and are only 50 m (55 yds) from the seafront. ⓐ Calle El Jable, Callao Salvaje ⓣ 922 70 023 ⓦ www.atlantic-holiday.com

Fiesta Hotel Oasis Paraíso ££ This hotel is good value for money and has activities for all ages. ⓐ Avenida Adeje 300 Playa Paraíso ⓣ 922 741 049 ⓦ www.fiestahotelgroup.com

PUERTO DE SANTIAGO

Hotel Barceló Santiago ££ A nice quiet part of the island and only five minutes' walk from the beach, this hotel offers impressive views of the neighbouring island Gomera and the Los Gigantes cliffs. ⓐ La Hondura 8, Puerto de Santiago ⓣ 922 860 912 ⓦ www.barcelosantiago.com

LOS GIGANTES

Apartments El Hotelito £ This much sought after range of apartments is located next to Playa Los Gigantes and the marina. The three-storey block has a typical Canarian feel and comes complete with a sea water swimming pool designed by César Manrique. ⓐ Calle Poblado Marinero, Los Gigantes ⓣ 922 860 966 ⓦ www.elhotelito.com

PLAYA DE LA ARENA

Hotel Playa Arena ££–£££ This hotel offers splendid views of the island Gomera, is situated only a few metres from a little volcanic beach and boasts soundproof rooms. ⓐ Calle Lajial 4, Playa de la Arena ⓣ 922 862 920 ⓦ www.springhoteles.com

PUERTO DE LA CRUZ

Hotel Miramar ££ The hotel sits perched on a hill, in the heart of the Taoro Park: an area of lush gardens, fountains and exotic plants. It's quiet but still very close to the town centre. All rooms come with a balcony or terrace and most have a splendid view of Mount Teide or the sea. ⓐ Parque Taoro ⓣ 922 384 811 ⓦ www.miramartf.com

Preparing to go

GETTING THERE

The cheapest way to get to Tenerife is to book a package holiday with one of the leading tour operators specialising in Canary Islands holidays. You should also check the Travel supplements of the weekend newspapers, such as the *Sunday Telegraph* and *The Sunday Times*. They often carry adverts for inexpensive flights, as well as classified adverts for privately owned villas and apartments to rent in most popular holiday destinations.

If your travelling times are flexible, and if you can avoid the school holidays, you can also find some very cheap last-minute deals using the websites for the leading holiday companies.

Many people are aware that air travel emits CO_2, which contributes to climate change. You may be interested in the possibility of lessening the environmental impact of your flight through the charity Climate Care, which offsets your CO_2 by funding environmental projects around the world. Visit ⓦ www.climatecare.org

TOURISM AUTHORITY

There are of course many websites covering the Canaries and Tenerife – the official Government site carries comprehensive listings and does some good offers and promotions.
ⓦ www.turismodecanarias.com/en/main.php

Also see the Island government's website ⓦ www.tenerife.es
ⓘ 902 00 31 21

BEFORE YOU LEAVE

Holidays should be about fun and relaxation, so avoid last minute panics and stress by making your preparations well in advance.

It is not necessary to have inoculations to travel in Europe, but you should make sure you and your family are up to date with the basics, such as tetanus. It is a good idea to pack a small first-aid kit to carry with you containing plasters, antiseptic cream, travel sickness pills, insect repellent and/or bite relief cream, antihistamine tablets, upset stomach

TRAVEL INSURANCE

Have you got sufficient cover for your holiday? Check that your policy covers you adequately for loss of possessions and valuables, for activities you might want to try – such as scuba diving, horse-riding, or water sports – and for emergency medical and dental treatment, including flights home if required. The European Health Insurance Card (EHIC) replaces the old E111 form, which enables you to reclaim the costs of some medical treatment incurred while travelling in EU countries. For information and an application form, enquire at the post office or visit Ⓦ www.dh.gov.u/travellers

remedies and painkillers. Sun lotion can be more expensive in Tenerife than in the UK so it is worth taking a good selection especially of the higher factor lotions if you have children with you, and don't forget after-sun cream as well. If you are taking prescription medicines, ensure that you take enough for the duration of your visit – you may find it impossible to obtain the same medicines in Tenerife. It is also worth having a dental check-up before you go.

ENTRY FORMALITIES

The most important documents you will need are your tickets and your passport. Check well in advance that your passport is up to date and has at least three months left to run (six months is even better). All children, including newborn babies, need their own passport now, unless they are already included on the passport of the person they are travelling with. It generally takes at least three weeks to process a passport renewal. This can be longer in the run-up to the summer months. For the latest information on how to renew your passport and the processing times call the Passport Agency on ☎ 0870 521 0410, or access their website Ⓦ www.ukpa.gov.uk

If you are thinking of hiring a car while you are away, you will need to have your UK driving licence with you. If you want more than one driver for the car, the other drivers must have their licence too.

MONEY

Like mainland Spain and much of Europe, the Canary Islands use the euro. You may need some currency before you go, especially if your flight gets you to your destination at the weekend or late in the day after the banks have closed. Traveller's cheques are the safest way to carry cash because the money will be refunded if the cheques are lost or stolen. To buy traveller's cheques or exchange money at a bank you may need to give up to a week's notice, depending on the quantity of currency you require. You can exchange money at the airport before you depart. Credit cards are widely accepted in the Canaries but make sure that your credit, charge and debit cards are up to date.

CLIMATE

Tenerife is known as the land of eternal spring and bad weather is rare. Generally you will find hot sunshine with temperatures in winter between 20 and 25°C and between 25 and 30°C during the summer months. You will mainly need to take beach wear but include a light jacket for the cooler evenings. If you are planning a trip to Mount Teide, a sweater may also be in order as the weather can be much cooler so high up. If you are staying in a four or five star hotel, the hotel may require men to wear long trousers and shirt sleeves for dinner.

BAGGAGE ALLOWANCE

Baggage allowances vary according to the airline, destination and the class of travel, but 20 kg (44 lb) per person is the norm for luggage that is carried in the hold (it usually tells you what the weight limit is on your ticket). You are also allowed one item of cabin baggage weighing no more than 5 kg (11 lb), and measuring 46 by 30 by 23 cm (18 by 12 by 9 inches). In addition, you can usually carry your duty-free purchases, umbrella, handbag, coat, camera, etc, as hand baggage. Large items – surfboards, golf-clubs, collapsible wheelchairs and pushchairs – are usually charged as extras and it is a good idea to let the airline know in advance that you want to bring these.

🔵 *Remember to wear a jumper if hiking at Cañadas del Teide*

During your stay

AIRPORTS

There are two airports in Tenerife. The south airport (Reina Sofia) is where all international flights, as well as some domestic ones, arrive and depart. This airport is located approximately 15 minutes' drive from the main tourist resorts of Playa de las Américas and Los Cristianos.

The airport located in the north of the island (Los Rodeos) caters for international and domestic Spanish flights although British charter flights to this airport operate only in winter. It is located about 20 minutes' drive from the resort of Puerto de la Cruz. From here you can get flights to all the other Canary Islands via Binter airlines. The south airport also has some flights to other islands. Journey times vary between 20 minutes and an hour.

COMMUNICATIONS
Public telephones

There are many telephone booths dotted around where you can make calls with credit cards or using coins. Please be warned that if you are using coins, you will need lots of them. Calls can also be made from your hotel room but this is an expensive option. The local operator can be reached by dialling 1003.

TELEPHONING ABROAD

To call an overseas number from the Canaries, dial 00 followed by the country code (UK = 44, Ireland = 353), then the area code (leaving out the initial zero) and the number.

TELEPHONING TENERIFE

To call Tenerife from the UK, dial 00 34 then the nine-digit number – there's no need to wait for a dialling tone.

Telefonica, the main telephone company, has several kiosks in tourist areas where you can make metered calls and then pay an attendant after you have finished.

Post offices
Post offices (*correos*) are open Mon–Fri 09.00–14.00 and Saturday 09.00–13.00. Stamps (*sellos*) for letters and cards to the UK cost 60 centimos. Stamps can normally also be bought at shops which sell postcards. Post boxes are usually yellow. If there are two slots in which to post cards, choose the one which says 'alextranjero'.

DRESS CODES
Unless you are visiting a casino or a very smart restaurant, there is no need to dress up. Topless sunbathing is allowed anywhere on Tenerife and there are three designated naturist beaches at Playa de la Tejita (El Médano), Playa de los Patos (La Orotava) and Playa de las Gaviotas (Santa Cruz de Tenerife).

ELECTRICITY
Voltage is 220 V, and two-pin sockets are used – UK appliances will need an adaptor. Power cuts can still happen particularly during the winter months, so a torch can sometimes come in handy.

If you are considering buying electrical appliances to take home, always check that they will work in the UK before you buy.

EMERGENCIES
The biggest chain of private hospitals in Spain is USP, their main centre is in Adeje but they also have a 24-hour medical post in Puerto Santiago.

WHAT TO DO IN AN EMERGENCY
The number for general emergencies is 112. For the police: 091 Ask your rep for advice if you have to attend a police station and take your passport.

USP Hospital Costa Adeje
ⓐ Urb. San Eugenio. Edf. Garajonay, Adeje ☏ 922 75 26 26
ⓦ www.uspcostaadeje.com

CONSULATE

The British Consulate in Tenerife is located in Santa Cruz, at Plaza Weyler 8 (☏ 922 28 68 63 ☏ 922 28 99 03). The consulate is located directly above the Barclays Bank and its opening hours are 09.00–13.00 Monday to Friday.

The Irish Consulate opens 09.00–13.00 Monday to Friday and can be contacted on ☏ 922 24 56 71.

If you are a British National and your passport is lost or stolen whilst in Tenerife, you will have to get an emergency replacement passport from the consulate. Due to the large number of illegal immigrants who enter the Canary Islands by sea from Africa, many of whom then try to enter the UK by air, the requirements imposed on airlines by UK immigration authorities are very strict. Failure to obtain a replacement passport may mean that the airlines will not allow you to travel.

Should you need to get a replacement passport, you will first need to obtain a police report from the National Police (Policia Nacional) in the town where it was lost/stolen. There is also a 24-hour number (with English translators) where reports can be made over the phone. A reference number is given and you can then collect the report within 24 hours from your nearest police station. The number for this service is ☏ 902 102 112. Once you have your police report, take it to the consulate along with four passport-sized photos and a letter of confirmation of identity from your tour operator. The consulate charges approximately £55 for this service. You may be able to claim some of this cost back via your holiday insurance.

GETTING AROUND

Car hire and driving One of the best and cheapest ways to get around the island is to hire a car. However, there is a large choice of car hire companies so it is best to shop around first. Don't just check the price and go for the cheapest though, but also check what each price covers and make sure you have sufficient insurance.

When driving you must always carry your passport, driving licence and the car hire contract. If you fail to produce these documents immediately spot fines can be issued. If your driving licence states that you wear glasses, you should carry a spare pair in the car as well.

Should your hire car break down, most reputable companies will have an assistance number that you can call. This is one of the things you should check when shopping around for the best deal. Please note that it is Canarian law that all cars must carry two red emergency triangles (these are generally found in the boot). Should you break down, you should place one a little way behind your car and the other a little way in front to warn other drivers. Failure to do so may result in an on-the-spot fine.

Most cars now take unleaded petrol (*sin plomo*). Diesel is 'gas oil'. Don't forget to check with the hire company which type of fuel the car uses before driving away.

Rules of the road Drive on the right, and note that seat belts must be worn, and drink-drive laws are strict. Police carry out random checks and may impose on-the-spot fines. Carry your licence, photo ID and car hire contract with you. Speed cameras are in operation; limits vary from 50kph (30mph) in built-up zones to 120 kph (75 mph) on motorways – watch for the signs. Pay-and-display systems operate at certain hours wherever there are blue lines marked on the roads, so keep a good supply of coins handy for the machines. Parking is not allowed in yellow spaces. In towns, you must park in the same direction as the flow of traffic. Note that motorway exits are demarcated by 'Km', followed by the number of the exit (i.e. Km 27).

Public transport Scheduled bus services are operated by Titsa and cover a large variety of routes. There are bus stations in the main resorts of Los Cristianos, Playa de las Americas and Puerto de la Cruz as well as many bus stops dotted around. Services are cheap and frequent and timetables are normally displayed at all stops and stations. The Canarian word for a bus is *guagua*, which is pronounced 'wah wah'.

From the ferry port in Los Cristianos you can get ferries to the neighbouring island of La Gomera that take about 45 minutes. Also from Los Cristianos you can reach the islands of La Palma and El Hierro.

Santa Cruz de Tenerife also has a ferry port where you can catch a hydrofoil or ferry to towns on the other Canary Islands.

The only passenger and vehicle shipping line to operate a regular service between Tenerife and the mainland is Transmediterranea which operates one service a week between Cadiz and Tenerife. The UK agent for Transmediterranea is Southern Ferries. ⓐ First Floor, 179 Piccadilly, London W1V 9DB ① 020 7491 4968 ① 020 7491 3502

Please note that cars can be taken on all ferries and some hydrofoils but check with your car hire company first as you will probably not be insured to take the car off the island. If this is the case, cars can usually be hired in the ferry ports at your destinations.

Taxis These are fairly cheap. Most taxis on the island are white estate cars and have an SP plate on. A taxi which is available to hire will have a green light on the roof.

HEALTH, SAFETY AND CRIME

Food and drink precautions Mains water is perfectly safe, but tastes awful due to the high volcanic mineral content. Buy bottled water for general drinking, tea, coffee, etc. It's best to buy bottled water from the supermarkets. The cost of a 5-litre bottle is around €1. There are two types available, *agua con gas* is sparkling mineral water and the more common *agua sin gas* still water. Avoid ice cubes unless you are sure it is made from bottled water, this includes ice in drinks.

Health care Standards of medical care are high on Tenerife. Although EU residents are entitled to some reciprocal health care in the Canaries, travellers are advised to carry an EHIC (see page 113), which entitles them to medical treatment in any medium-sized state clinic or hospital. Please note that most hospitals and clinics in Tenerife are private. Make sure you have adequate medical insurance before you travel; all the island hospitals will accept British insurance and they all have English-speaking staff. Pharmacies: a *farmacia* (chemist) can be recognised by a large

BEACH SAFETY

In summer, many beaches have life guards and a flag safety system. Other beaches may be safe for swimming but there are unlikely to be lifeguards or life-saving amenities available. It is important to bear in mind that the strong winds that develop in the hotter months can quickly change what appears to be a safe beach into a not-so-safe one, and some can have strong currents the further out that you go.

- **Red flag** = dangerous – no swimming, even if other people are doing so. Freak waves may drag you off promenades or rocks.
- **Yellow** = good swimmers only; apply caution.
- **Green** = safe bathing conditions for all.

green cross on a white background. Most of these keep shop hours, but there is always a 24-hour rota system for emergencies. The nearest *farmacia de guardia* (duty chemist) will be listed on the door. At night, only prescription medicines are dispensed.

Crime levels You should always take advantage of the safety deposit box facility in your hotel even though this usually carries a charge. This will protect your belongings and also satisfy your insurance company that you have taken 'due care' of your belongings should you need to make a claim.

Car theft sometimes occurs so it is best not to leave any valuables in a parked car. Anything that you do leave in the car is best left out of sight.

Violent crime is rare on the island but opportunistic thefts (particularly from unsuspecting tourists) do sometimes occur. Remember to keep your hand on all purses and wallets, particularly in crowded areas such as markets.

If you are out in the main nightlife centres, keep your wits about you and do not leave bags or purses unattended at any time. Never stray on to the beach at night as this is a common place where opportunistic thefts occur. At night, taxis should be taken around the resort and back to your hotel.

There are two security forces in Tenerife, the local police and the civil guard or *policia local* and *guardia civil*. The *guardia civil* have green uniforms with green markings on their cars, the *policia local* – blue uniforms with blue markings on their cars. Only telephone the police if you need their assistance to stop a crime in progress. The police here speak very little English so unless you can talk to them in Spanish, simply let them know where you are and they will come straight to you to sort out any problem.

If you are the victim of theft whilst here and are covered by insurance, you need a police report to make a claim. You also need a police report for a duplicate passport. The first person you should notify is your holiday representative if you've booked through a tour operator. They may be able to warn other guests and, more importantly, they can arrange for someone to go with you to the police station to make the report. If you haven't a representative to report to, try the reception of the apartment complex or hotel that you're staying at. They can arrange for someone to go with you, although there may be a fee to pay if they contact a professional translator for you.

If you're driving a car, as well as papers for the car you must always have your driving licence and passport with you. If you're stopped by the police and can't provide all of these, you will suffer an on-the-spot fine of anything up to 300 euros. If you're speeding more than 20 miles over the legal limit, expect a larger fine. Finally, do not (under any circumstances) lose your temper with either police force, argue with them or shout at them. You will regret it

MEDIA

English-speaking visitors will not feel cut off from home in Tenerife. There are a plethora of newspapers and magazines catering for the ex-pat community – and of course the main papers from England (for a price). Power FM and Gold FM are the two big English radio stations in Tenerife and Satellite television is widely available.

OPENING HOURS

Banks are generally open Monday to Friday 08.30–14.00 and on Saturday 09.00–13.00 in winter only. Shops and businesses are generally open Monday to Friday 09.00–13.00 and 16.00–20.00, and Saturday 09.00–13.00. Within large resorts these hours are often extended and some shops may even open on a Sunday.

Most chemists (*farmacia*) obey the same opening hours as shops. However, there is always a duty chemist (*farmacia de guardia*) open until late and during siesta time in every area. For details of the duty chemist, check in the window of any chemist. For travellers staying in the south of the island there is a 24-hour chemist open every day of the year just opposite the Veronicas nightlife area in Playa de las Americas.

Restaurants in tourist areas generally open from 13.00 until late. In quieter areas they may close after lunch at around 16.00 and reopen at 19.30 or 20.00. The Canarian people rarely eat before 21.00 and restaurants are less crowded before that time.

Most museums open only in the morning – usually between 09.00 and 14.00. Museums are usually free on Sundays. The main public holidays in Tenerife are: 1 January, 6 January, 1 May, 15 August, 12 October, 1 November and 25 December. In addition to these there are several other public holidays whose date changes every year, the main one of these being Carnival whose date depends on Easter. There are also many local holidays when whole towns will close down for a day or so.

RELIGION

In Tenerife, as in mainland Spain, the main religion is Catholicism and almost all the towns and cities, including tourist resorts, have churches where mass is frequently held.

TIME DIFFERENCES

There is no difference between Tenerife and the UK at any time.

New York is four hours behind, San Francisco seven. Sydney is eleven hours ahead.

TIPPING

Many restaurants include a service charge in the bill and so there is no need to tip unless you have received exceptionally good service and wish to show your appreciation. If service is not included, an average tip is considered to be 10 per cent of the bill. This applies to services, taxis, restaurants and bars.

TOILETS

Public toilets are generally found around the beach areas in the tourist resorts. Usually there will be a charge for use of these facilities.

TRAVELLERS WITH DISABLITIES

Most of the main tourist areas have adapted their pavements to enable wheelchair access. Very few hotels actually have adapted rooms and facilities though. If in doubt whether the accommodation or resort you would like to book is suitable, please check with your tour operator.

There are several companies that hire electric mobility scooters and wheelchairs and also organise excursions and airport transfers: **Active Mobility** 922 78 97 07 www.activemobility-tenerife.com **LeRo** 922 75 02 89 www.lero.net and **Orange** 922 79 73 55 www.orangebadge.com

The island government webpage has information on beaches and accessibility issues. www.portalturismoaccesible.org

One of the municipalities with very advanced services is Arona. Their web page has detailed information on Playa de Las Vistas, where there are trained helpers and special equipment to enable bathing in the sea. www.arona.org

The website also has a downloadable guidebook containing an enormous amount of information on facilities at beaches, hotels, restaurants and shopping centres.

ACKNOWLEDGEMENTS

We would like to thank all the photographers, picture libraries and organisations for the loan of the photographs reproduced in this book, to whom copyright in the photograph belongs:

Bigstockphotos (page 26); Getty Images (pages 8, 36, 76, 90, 115); Jon Smith (pages 96, 107, 109); Pictures Colour Library Ltd (pages 13, 22, 24, 55, 80, 84); Thomas Cook (pages 1, 5, 33, 35, 40, 44, 47, 48, 50, 52, 60, 64, 67, 75, 93, 103); World Pictures/Photoshot (pages 10–11, 30, 32, 39, 94).

Project editor: Tom Willsher
Layout: Donna Pedley
Proofreader: Amanda Learmonth
Indexer: Marie Lorimer

Send your thoughts to
books@thomascook.com

- Found a beach bar, peaceful stretch of sand or must-see sight that we don't feature?

- Like to tip us off about any information that needs a little updating?

- Want to tell us what you love about this handy little guidebook and more importantly how we can make it even handier?

Then here's your chance to tell all! Send us ideas, discoveries and recommendations today and then look out for your valuable input in the next edition of this title.

Email to the above address or write to:
HotSpots Series Editor, Thomas Cook Publishing, PO Box 227, Unit 9, Coningsby Road, Peterborough PE3 8SB, UK.